TIMELESS WISDOM

The Best of Dr. Frank Crane's Four-Minute Essays

TIMELESS WISDOM

The Best of Dr. Frank Crane's Four-Minute Essays

Compiled by
K. R. TALBOT

CFI
SPRINGVILLE, UT

ISBN 13:978-1-59955-029-9

Published by CFI, an imprint of Cedar Fort, Inc., 2373 W. 700 S., Springville, UT, 84663
Distributed by Cedar Fort, Inc. www.cedarfort.com

LIBRARY OF CONGRESS CATALOGING-IN-PUBLICATION DATA

Crane, Frank, 1861-1928.
  Timeless wisdom : the best of Dr. Frank Crane's four-minute essays / compiled by K.R. Talbot.
    p. cm.
  ISBN 978-1-59955-029-9 (acid-free paper)
  I. Talbot, K. R., 1983- II. Title. III. Title: Best of Dr. Frank Crane's four-minute essays.

PS3505.R27T56 2007
808.84'9--dc22

2007009046

Cover design by Nicole Williams
Cover design © 2007 by Lyle Mortimer
Typeset by Kammi Rencher

Printed in the United States of America

10 9 8 7 6 5 4 3 2 1

Printed on acid-free paper

A Word about This Book

The essays in this book were written around the turn of the twentieth century. They reflect the language and the sentiments of the times. There are also a number of words and phrases used in this book that have either fallen out of use or whose meanings have changed, either slightly or dramatically, since the time these essays were written.

Table of Contents

Foreword

It seems amazing to me that so much—and so little—has changed in just the last one hundred years of our history. The turn of the twentieth century brought electricity, aviation, the motorcar, radio, and advances in physics, psychology, and women's rights. Racism ran rampant, gambling was illegal, and Prohibition was brought into effect in 1920. The world was on the brink of World War I—a war after which we would never be the same.

A century later, we have come far and seen more war, more advances in science and technology, a reduction of racism, and vast improvements in women's rights; we now rely on computers do to our work, Internet and cell phones to communicate, and quick and comfortable vehicles for transportation. And yet—as people, in our values, our personalities, our thoughts—how much have we really changed?

Perhaps the thing that I first noticed when I read Dr. Crane's work was that even though his world was so different from mine, the ideas and morals he presented were not. In spite of all the years, all the advances in technology, and the vast differences in culture, our sense of values hasn't changed. People continue to find true happiness the same way now that they did then. And although in many ways the crimes, the sins, and the sorrows we have, have changed, the roots of all these have not. And they may never.

Dr. Frank Crane knew this. A Presbyterian minister in his younger years, Dr. Crane became known for his newspaper columns. One of the most widely read columnists of his time, Dr. Crane wrote on the common problems of the human race. His simple yet powerful words earned him devoted readers from coast to coast, and especially in the eastern United States. A popular speaker and gifted editor, he brought hope, peace, and patriotism during the dark days of World War I. Throughout his life, his staunch adherence to good values and positive thinking had a powerful impact on the lives of countless Americans.

Just over a decade after Dr. Crane's death, World War II broke out in Europe. Others, such as C. S. Lewis and Winston Churchill, arose to encourage the Allies through that time, and the name of Frank Crane slowly faded from the public consciousness. Today, his words live on, mostly in the form of popular quotes, scattered throughout books and over the Internet.

Strange, how much—and yet how little—can change in just one century. Nearly a hundred years ago, everyone knew the name of Frank Crane. Today, few do. Yet whether we know his name or not, the moral issues he wrote on were the same then as they are now.

Timeless wisdom cannot be fully lost.

—K. R. Talbot

What I Write Is My Tombstone

Volume 1

I have lately been going about in Rome and its environs. It is preeminently the land of the Tombstone. Rome should be called that, if it ever changes its name, and if the title had not been preempted by a town in Arizona. There are tombs everywhere; tombs in the church floors, in the wall, under the high alters. All about are tombs of emperors and kings. All futile. All pillaged, empty, like eyeless sockets. The poor, powdered dust of the magnificent ones has been sifted to find their finger-rings.

The only real tomb is a book. Men of letters are the only genuine aristocracy; kings and thrones, in the landscape of history, are only located by their relation to the men who write. Napoleon, it has been said, will be remembered as a contemporary of Goethe.

The glory of Julius and Augustus is ashes; the golden house of Nero a subterranean cavern, damp and mossy; "the boast of heraldry, the pomp of power," are swept aside; but Horace with liquid syllables built himself "a monument more lasting than brass"; and Homer, Dante, and Shakespeare live on, green as perennial trees.

As for me, let my bones and flesh be burned, and the ashes dropped in the moving waters, and if my name shall live at all, let it be found among books, the only garden of forget-me-nots, the only human device for perpetuating this personality.

THE OLD-AGE DISEASE

Boston, said the funny man, is not a locality; Boston is a state of mind. To those who have experienced Boston this is a truth that needs not to be proved.

With equal accuracy it may be said that old age is not a number of years; it is a state of mind.

It has been observed that a woman is as old as she looks, and a man is as old as he feels; as a matter of fact, both are as old as they think.

There is no need of anybody growing old. For age is entirely a disease of the soul, a condition of ill health, which with reasonable caution may be avoided. It is no more necessary than measles, which the world once thought everyone ought to have; now we know better.

The human being begins existence as a vigorous animal, whose body naturally weakens with time and finally perishes. The body runs its course, "ripes and ripes, and rots and rots," like an apple or any other organized growth of matter. Hence of course there is a decrepitude of one's frame.

But this is not at all true of the mind. All things in nature, from mushrooms to oaks, from insects to elephants, and even mountains and suns and systems, have their periods of growth, maturity, and decay. The mind, however, has no such law. It is the "one exception" as Mark Hopkins called it.

And the mind is the real man. And the mind can be as young at ninety as it is at twenty-one.

Asking ourselves what it is that makes youthfulness, we discover the answer to be that it consists in three things:

Work, growth, and faith. So long as life functions in these three ways it is young. When any or more of these elements fall off we are old.

By work is meant an active participation in the interests of humankind. Notice how the boy cannot be idle, he wants to be at something, he burns to play the game.

Idleness or aloofness is the essence of growing old. The businessman who "retires" and devotes himself to doing nothing is committing suicide.

John Bigelow recently died at the age of ninety-five, and up to the last retained his interest in affairs.

It is work that keeps men young, more than play. No man should give up selling dry-goods if that is his life business, unless he has found some other business equally congenial and interesting.

I know a woman of eighty, mother of eleven grown children, who is as young as any of them, for she declines to be shelved.

The way to stay young is to keep in the game.

Secondly, growth. That is to say, mind-growth. Let the mind be always learning, alert for new truth, eager for new accomplishments.

It is when one's intellect closes, ceases to learn, and becomes an onlooker that old age sets in. How many old people impress you as beyond teachableness! They have settled everything, religion, politics, philosophy.

You can't teach an old dog new tricks, but because he will not learn new tricks is exactly the reason the dog is old.

It is when one takes up the study of Greek at seventy, or at eighty begins to investigate psychology, that his mind breathes spring air.

As long as a mind is teachable, open, and inquiring, it is young.

There ought to be special schools for people of sixty and over. Who goes to school keeps young.

Lastly, faith, not intellectual assent to any statement (which operation is no more to do with faith than sole-leather), but a general belief in men and things; confidence; settled, abiding courage and cheer.

Faith in one's self, in one's destiny, in mankind, in the universe and in Him who manages it—this is youth's peculiar liquor.

Doubt is the very juice of senility. Cynicism, pessimism, and despair are the dust that blows from a dried-up soul.

And faith is not something over which you have no control; it is a cultivable thing, it is a habit.

So long as one keeps at work, continues to learn, and has faith, he is young.

Whoever does not work, does not learn, and has no faith, is old even at thirty. Old age is a state of mind.

ALL NOISE IS WASTE

Power is a curious and much misunderstood thing. Noise and display, which are commonly thought to indicate it, in reality are indications of its absence.

All show of force is a sign of weakness. Loud talking is a sign of a consciousness that one's reasoning is feeble. When one shrieks it means that he knows or suspects that what he says does not amount to much, and it irritates him. Profanity comes from a limited vocabulary.

A country is poor in proportion to its fighting spirit. A nation habitually peaceful is hardest to conquer. It was the United States that settled with the Barbary pirates.

In advertisements, a persistent over-statement will in time destroy all confidence. Even here the strongest, most impressive thing, in the long run, is modesty.

Power is in inverse ratio to noise, as a rule.

The strongest being conceivable is God. And He is so modest, quiet, and hidden that many people refuse to believe there is a God. He never blusters. Hence humbugs cannot understand how He exists.

The most powerful material thing in our range of experience is the sun, the source of all earth-forces. Yet the sun's pull, energy, and radiation are silent. It raises billions of tons of water daily from the ocean with less noise than an April thunderstorm.

"The greatest things have need to be said most simply," remarked a Frenchman; "they are spoiled by emphasis."

ANGER

Volume 9

There is no use telling you, son, not to get angry; no use telling any red-blooded man that.

Indignation is a natural flame that spurts up in the mind, upon certain occasions, as surely as gasoline explodes at a lighted match.

All I say is—wait!

Don't do anything till your heat is gone. Don't say words, nor pass judgments, until your brain has cooled down.

For most anger is the irritation of offended vanity.

We think a lot of our opinion, and when one sneers at it, it is as if he threw mud on our white duck trousers.

We have a high notion of the respect due us, and when it is intimated that we are nobody we want to smash something to show we are somebody.

We are never angry, save when our pride is hurt.

Anger is self-esteem on fire.

So, flare up, if you must, swear and break the furniture; it may do you good; but go up to your room to indulge in this relief, lock the door, and stay there until the storm blows over.

Never write a letter while you are angry. Lay it aside. In a few days you can come back at your offender much more effectually.

Don't transact business in heat. When you are "mad clean through" it is your sore egotism that is operating, and acts prompted by egotism are usually ridiculous. Hang up the matter for a few days, and come to it again when your intelligence is not upset by your feelings.

One of the best things to say is nothing. When you answer a man he gets your measure; when you keep still you have him guessing.

The cool man, who has himself under control, always has the advantage over the hot man.

Even if you have to lick a man you can do much better if your head is clear of anger fumes. Wrath may lend a little extra punch to your blows, but self-control will plant them to better effect.

Anger dulls your efficiency. What you do goes wild. You have a lot of energy, but no accuracy.

Anger dims your eye. You see vividly, but what you see is not so.

Anger makes chaos in your thought. You are a crazy man. What you think in the egotism of anger you will pay for in the humiliation of saner moments.

Few good deeds have been done in anger, while all manner of crimes are due to the intemperance of wrath, such as blows, murders, and war, "the sum of all villainies."

The first and greatest lesson for you to learn, son, is to control your temper, and, if your nature is touchy, to resolve to take no action until the blood is cooled.

ANGER POISON

All the poisons are not kept in chained bottles on drug-store shelves.

All the cases of strange illness and wasting are not due to subtle drops from India nor mysterious powders sold by old witches.

And all the shocking deaths are not the result of taking tablets of bichloride of mercury thinking they are of aspirin.

The commonest, deadliest, and most dreadful poisons are those we carry around with us. They are contained in our mind.

There is no doubt about the injurious effects of certain emotions upon the body. They are as well authenticated as the operation of henbane or arsenic.

The exudation of sweat-glands, for instance, has been analyzed, and certain strong feelings have been shown to produce certain definite injurious secretions.

Anger is one state which produces diseased conditions, as headache, loss of appetite, deranged digestion, even syncope.

In one instance the anger of a mother had such an effect upon her suckling child that it died in paroxysms.

Not only the occasional outburst of anger, but those states we might call chronic anger, such as impatience, petulance, irritability, bad temper, and the like, produce as clear forms of intoxication (poisoning) as alcohol.

Many cases of chronic indigestion, nervousness, morbidity, and hypochondria are attributable to nothing but slow anger poison.

If one can clean the harmful ferments out of his body by a dose of salts or by the use of bran and oil, he can also cleanse his system of far more toxic contents by forgiving his enemies every night before he goes to bed, by daily purging his consciousness of all hates, resentments, and grudges.

Anger is sometimes unavoidable, as when we witness or hear of some outrageous act of injustice or cruelty. But if we must have it, let it be quick and soon over. For when it remains in us it is we who suffer, and not our adversary.

It unnerves our hand, blinds our vision, impairs our judgment, and when it leaps to vengeance invariably overleaps, bringing to us regret and remorse in lieu of satisfaction. "Remember," wrote Lord Chesterfield, "there are but two procedures in the world to a gentlemen and a man of parts: either extreme politeness or knocking down."

And mighty good advice it is from the old worldly-wise philosopher. For anger that is balked or impotent, if kept lurking in the mind, settles into a slow poison.

It distorts the features and makes even a handsome face ugly, gives a vicious twist to the smile and a forbidding cast to the eye.

It distorts our thoughts. We become unpleasant companions to ourselves, and from ourselves there is no escape.

It upsets sleep, disturbs the simple delights of eating and drinking, degrades our work, and spoils our play.

I do not say, "Don't get angry," but "Don't stay angry."

What has happened to you has happened to all men.
The question is, will you cull from it flowers or thorns?
—THE ART OF HAPPY MEMORY

AROUND THE CORNER

What's around the corner? Something. Whatever it is, I used to be terribly afraid of it, when a boy.

When I would take a girl home at night after meeting, I would walk out in the street a little, lest if I kept on the sidewalk I would be so close that Something around the Corner could get me. Nothing ever did jump out and grab me, never a ghost, or a booger-man, or a murderer, or anything, though I expected and feared [it] all those boy-years.

And since I have grown up I have discovered that Something around the Corner is believed in by most mortals. It may be accident or disease or loss or disgrace—or that old fellow himself who lurks around the corner for all of us, and will get us every one someday—Death.

The Thing around the Corner, it is the skeleton at the feast, the shadow on our sunny day, the nightmare of our sleep, the concealed weapon of destiny, the vague enemy that will not let us bivouac in peace, but makes us always keep our pickets out alert for stealthy attack.

And yet the good things of life are around the Corner. Happiness hides there and springs laughing at us. And the little things that make hearts bright and days glad. Ten of these blessed things have

come upon us unaware, to one of them that we have sought and found.

Love, for instance. Don't you remember how it was with you when it came to you that she really loved you? That wonderful, divine creature, the pearl of the world, that radiant one, the latchet of whose shoes you were not worthy to unloose—what could she see in so commonplace a mucker as you? O miracle of miracles!

Then there's Christmas, corner of all corners, with what amazing secrets and what crowded bevy of giggles and whispers and loving thoughts!

But especially the little things are they that make the sum of our contentment, and they are nearly all surprises. If we could foresee them we wouldn't appreciate them.

It's not the big Olympian gods that love us most; it's the little fairies of circumstance, the elves and pyxies of happy accident that flutter along the ways of men.

The best things of life come unexpected upon you. From the time when you were presented with your first pair of trousers, or Uncle Ed brought you home a toy pistol, down to just yesterday when a friend paid you back the ten dollars you lent him and never expected to see again, and all through your life, your successes in business, your rarest friends, your most palatable food, your most enjoyable excursions, your most interesting books, the remarks someone made about you that most tickled your vanity, the most welcome visitors—almost all of them were not planned and worked for, but jumped at you from around the corner.

And around that last Corner, where we turn to travel the unknown, I do not believe there hides some grisly thing of evil, but a smiling-faced One, with welcome in His hands and the Morning Star for me.

THE ART OF HAPPY MEMORY

Volume 10

The most significant step a mind takes is that wherein it realizes that it can control its own operation; when it learns that it can command those things in itself commonly considered automatic.

And in nothing does this appear with such striking results to happiness as in the discovery of one's power to manage his memory.

Most people think they remember what they remember, and that is all there is to it. But it is possible to make memory a servant, and restrain its mastery.

In Italy a rare motto was found by Hazlitt upon a sun-dial: *Horas non numero nisi serenas*—"I mark only the shining hours."

The man whose increase of contentment is most assured, as he grows older, is the one who has discovered how to enjoy his past.

To many of us the past is always sad. We turn from it with impatience. "Man never is, but always to be, blest." Naturally this habit of mind sees in the ever-shortening future nothing but tragedy. Accept, then, these hints on how to handle your past.

First, whatever it is, has been; it has brought you here. Your condition may not be all your impudent claims on the universe demand, but it might be worse. Better men than you are in jail, are stricken with unceasing pain. Better men than you have been hanged.

Out of the worst experiences you have had you may reap satisfaction. The dangers, sicknesses, accidents, and losses, one who understands the art of living finds in the recalling of even these a certain thankfulness. Is there not pleasure in recounting your narrow escape?

You have had your pangs and

pains; but the wise man knows that out of these have come his richest crops of understanding. Life has its stripes; but they are its healing.

The past is largely made by the present. If you are now soured and disappointed you are quite hopeless, for your diseased memory will go over your past and pick out from it only miserable things. But if you have adjusted yourself, if with a courageous heart you are trying to make the best of conditions as they are, your memory will aid you, and bring you stores of happy incidents.

Your past is the strongest asset of your present judgment. It is your best teacher. Only from it do you learn whatever shrewdness you have in dealing with events.

Learn to forgive yourself, not in folly, but in a sane charity. The things you did wrong, the failures and mistakes, consider them as part of that tutelage of destiny that goes toward your present equipment.

What has happened to you has happened to all men. The question is, will you cull from it flowers or thorns?

"Everything considered," says Renan, "there are few situations in the vast field of existence where the balance of debt and credit does not leave a little surplus of happiness."

We have crossed the years. We are here. We have escaped what perils! We have landed with what residue of wisdom and of hope!

BACKSLIDING

In certain conventicles a deal has been said about backsliding.

It is an experience we have all had.

Because backsliding is as much a characteristic of progress as forward-going. All growth is rhythmic. Periodicity is a method of life.

The tree backslides in winter. The most active man backslides once a day into sleep. There is no such thing in nature, among living things, as uninterrupted force. It is merely a mental concept, and does not exist in the world of realities.

Common sense therefore would indicate that we adjust ourselves to this law, and not fret under it.

It is important that mothers should realize this. Occasionally the child seems to slump, to forget all his morals and manners, and revert to savagery. Then is not the time to despair, and ask what is the use, and cry out that all one's efforts have come to naught. It is the time to wait, to be patient, until the spell is over, and the pendulum swings back. He will recover. All goodness as it proceeds must have little lapses of badness, and success must have little vacations of failure.

The teacher in her schoolroom, the businessman in his office, the artist and author in their creative work, the workman at whatever task, must feel the ebb and flow of efficiency, for all power has its tides.

Among the healthiest there are days they do not feel up to the mark, all optimists have now and then a dash of pessimism, the most holy cut up their didos once in a while (whether they admit it or not), and even criminals have their hours of good resolve.

And in a wider way the whole earth lumbers forward, now going on and now seeming to stand still or go back, but every generation of men sees mankind nearer to perfection.

Science never permanently recedes. Things learned can never be unlearned. And law and righteousness never retreat.

They have their backslidings. The world is just now backsliding mightily. But don't worry.

We are not going back, to stay, to the darkness of autocracy nor the dirty barbarity of militarism. If the filthy Prussians conquer the world, they couldn't keep it under. For the simple reason that mankind, as a whole, could not forget and lose all its training in decency, justice, and humanity, and acquiesce in the abominable tutelage of a race of fiends, any more than your child, no matter how wayward his backslidings, can utterly forget his decent parentage and upbringing.

Come what will, we will not cease our eternal creed:

"O yet we trust that somehow good
Will be the final goal of ill."

THE BETTER CONQUEST

Volume 2

It is well to conquer Germany, my soldier. But it is better to conquer yourself.

The Huns cannot hurt you half so badly as the inner enemies that devastate the soul.

The wounds of enemy bullets are honorable. But the wounds of your own unmastered weakness are scars of shame.

You are not doing all the giving in this contract between you and your country. To be sure, you give your time, your toil, your obedience, perhaps your life; but you are getting something in return, and something more than adventure, keep, insurance, and the satisfaction of duty done, for you are getting something as precious as life itself, as without it life is a dull and limping thing—you are getting discipline.

You will not only be taught how to obey your officers, you will learn how to obey yourself.

When you realize the pride and pleasure of instantly heeding your captain's command, you will find it but a short step to that finer pride and keener pleasure that come from quick and unquestioning obedience to the captain of your soul, whose name is Ought.

For the first of all virtues is the soldier virtue, promptly doing what we Ought to do.

Conscience is the soul's captain, and judgment and intelligence its lieutenants.

When orders come from these authorities the thoroughbred soul salutes and leaps to obey; it is the loose soul that argues.

Every soul has its Balaklava. Those that are noble ride forth in splendid carelessness of danger, "theirs not to reason why, theirs but to do and die."

There is hardship in military life. There is gruelling exertion, hunger, cold, heat, and always the possibility of peril. To the soul that finds no happiness but in the flesh-pots of self-indulgence, to the imagination that can revel only in the delights of dalliance, the soldier's career may be repulsive. But there is a better and manlier happiness that lies only through obstacles, and can only be found by conquest. This "stern joy that warriors feel" is worth all the feather beds of pampered ease.

This is what is meant by the saying that he that overcometh shall receive the crown. For if you set your teeth and lock your steeled will against self-pity, trample your fears and lusts ruthlessly under foot, and plunge resolutely on to the conquest of yourself, yours is the crown, the kingship of self, that divine peace that passeth understanding, which the cowards and slackers do not know, neither indeed can know.

Mobilize yourself, call every passion to the colors, bring every thought and longing to submission, put your mind and heart in military training, save your kindness and mercy for others, and when your soldiering is over you will find that you are more than a soldier, you will be a man.

Make up your mind to find the hidden joy that lies in discipline.

This is the better conquest.

THE BOY AND THE GANG

Volume 5

Most boys are more easily handled by wholesale than by retail.

Of all clannish creatures in time and space, the boy is probably the most clannish. The Assassins of the Orient, the McCanns of Scotland, the Nihilists of Russia, or the Chinese White Wolves, are no more devoted to their fellowcrafts than the boy to his gang.

About a certain age the boy-bud begins to separate from his parent-stem. Up till now he has had no individuality; it has been merged into the family. He has thought, believed, and acted as his brothers and sisters.

But there comes that day when he returns from his play, and it seems as if he were a new personality. He is changed. His mother is nonplussed. Grandma wants to know "whatever has come over the child." The pious aunt is shocked.

The cause is that the boy has made a new discovery. He has found a friend. It is almost as shatteringly wonderful when a boy experiences his first comradeship as when he first falls in love.

The parents cannot understand it. He seems to worship that Kelly boy. He talks like him, gestures like him, almost looks like him.

It is a wise parent that is careful to selected the child's "gang." It is almost as important as his family. For the gang instinct is very strong.

Boys that lie and steal elsewhere will be loyal to the gang. The gang-morals and gang-ideals are more binding on him than anything that teachers and Sunday school can supply.

For this reason boy-gangs should be selected carefully and encouraged. A week's tramp with a decent lot of Boy Scouts will do more good than a year's parental advice.

Do not imagine that you can repress the gang instinct in your boy. It is nature's calling. It is for you, as your boy's best friend, to help him find the right gang. For it is truer of him than of any of us grown-ups, that the best and worst of the individual is the company he plays with.

In the streets of heaven you will never blush to
think that you have forgiven too much.
—FORGET IT

The Boy or Girl That Quits School

Volume 8

Don't hustle. Think!

An ounce of intelligent getting ready is worth a pound of fussing.

Time spent in sharpening your axe counts as ten times of hacking and hewing.

It is certainly worthwhile to take aim before you shoot.

There is some good in keeping everlastingly at it, but a deal of humbug, too.

If you're doing a thing wrong, the more everlastingly you keep at it the worse you're off.

Nine-tenths of efficiency is preparedness.

If you are a boy, go through school. I have met thousands of men in my time, I never knew one to say he was sorry he went to school; I never knew one who had failed to finish his schooling that did not say he was sorry for it.

Of all fools on earth, the boy who will not take an education when he has a chance is the most sickening. He is deliberately handicapping himself in a race where he needs every advantage.

He is giving the other fellows odds when he needs for himself all the favorable conditions he can get.

He is laying up many an hour of humiliation for himself, days of regret, nights of bitter self-accusation.

He is pitting his immature judgment against the accumulated experience and wisdom of the whole human race.

He is indulging in weakness or laziness that he will pay for a hundred times over.

He is selling his birthright for a mess of pottage.

He is laying up shame and pain for all who are unfortunate enough to love him.

He is an ass.

He is a monumental, three-star, prize, blue-ribbon, exhibition ass.

He is an ass of the longest-eared and palest gray variety.

God help him, for he won't let anybody else!

If these few feeble remarks shall jolt any youth into a realization of the colossal mistake he is making in quitting school, I shall be happy.

We are opposed to corporal punishment and to all forms of violence; but if there is any one thing that makes us want to use a large, bumpy, hickory club, it is the boy or girl that will not go to school.

Of course some people have achieved success who never had any schooling. True. Some people also have got rich or famous who had but one leg or were blind. Shall we therefore lop off a leg or put out one eye?

THE CALL

Volume 6

You have as much sense as the next man. Use it. Rely on it. And it will grow.

You have two good hands, two good eyes, two good ears, your liver and lights are in good working order, you have just as good a physical machine as Vincent Astor. Use them.

You have as much faith as St. Francis ever had, if you'd use it.

You have as much hope and cheer as Mark Tapley. Use it.

You have as much strenuosity as Roosevelt. Use it.

You have as good an education as Rockefeller had.

You can read the same newspapers, magazines, and books Mr. Howells reads.

You can see the same pictures in the galleries that Charles Dana Gibson can see.

You have as many funny experiences as George Ade.

You have a pen and as much paper as Rudyard Kipling.

There's as much adventure calling you as ever called General Funston.

You have twenty-four hours a day, just the same as Woodrow Wilson.

What's the matter with you? Why don't you make good? All the wide seas want ships; where is yours?

The quarries are full of stone waiting to go into houses, the mines are gorged with ore, the forests are thick with building material.

Bridges need building, inventions are pleading to be born, the world is hungry for interesting books. Build, invent, write!

Every magazine editor is searching diligently in his mail for the real story; send one in.

Every business house is crying for salesmen, every woman wants a good husband, children want teachers; the demand for the right man everywhere is tremendous.

What seems to be your trouble?

What do you mean you have no chance?

Opportunity's knuckles are all skinned knocking at your door.

Farmers can't find laborers, housewives can't find cooks, theatrical managers can't find the right plays, churches can't find sufficient pastors.

The scarcest thing in this world is a man, a real man.

Fear is not bread of ignorance. It is the child of half-knowledge.

—THE CAMPAIGN AGAINST FEAR

THE CAPACITY TO FORGET

Listen!

The clock is about to strike. It is upon midnight, December the thirty-first. The year is dying. Its pulses grow fainter. But a little space now and it will be dead, dead and gone forever.

We will have to put it away with all the other dead things, good and bad, that have lived with us.

What a lot of burying there is to be done in this world, first and last! Some of them we are glad to get under the sod; our follies, for instance; our blunders, our acts of cowardice and meanness, our crass greeds and ugly lusts, our nasty egotisms, our absurd failures. Thank heaven there is a past, a big, yawning, capacious past for all such!

Thank heaven for forgetfulness, sweet, soothing forgetfulness! What a beautiful word *forget* is, in all its persons, moods, and tenses! Come, let us decline it, as the old clock clears its throat to say twelve.

I forget, thou wilt forget, he has forgotten; she might, could, would, or should forget; we shall or will have forgotten; you may forget; they, you, I, we, everybody, forget (imperative) right now a thousand and one little things and a few big things that have worked wretchedness in our hearts this year, like worms in the bud!

Forget it, little boy, that your father spoke sharply to you and pushed you from him but yesterday when you ran up eagerly with wide arms and a hundred smiles all at once. When I look at you now, asleep there in your bed, and your hand doubled up by your chubby cheek, I am amazed at my small patience, at my lack of greatness.

Forget it, woman of my heart, if ever one motion, gesture, glance, or thought of love from you started toward me and was frozen back. Forget! Don't forgive. When you forgive, the sting and swelling remain. Oh, if we could forget, and root the whole matter out, so that it should be as if it had never occurred!

There be those that say they can forgive but not forget. God pity 'em! I want a deeper pit than forgiveness to bury my dead vermin of trouble in.

The greater the soul the greater its power to forget. I would like a forgettery wide as the ocean, deep as hell. I want a forgetting apparatus overwhelming as a flood and clean as fire.

And when I come to go, let my prayer be Wordsworth's:

"Sweet Mercy! to the gates of
    Heaven
This minstrel lead, his sins forgiven;
The rueful conflict, the heart riven

With vain endeavor,
And memory of earth's bitter leaven
Effaced forever!"
Come! The clock strikes. It is low twelve. Let us set fire to the past year, and burn it over as a farmer his last year's stubble; and get ready for our spring planting.

THE CAMPAIGN AGAINST FEAR

Volume 7

The campaign against fear is the greatest movement of the race. Fear is not bread of ignorance. It is the child of half-knowledge. "A little knowledge is a dangerous thing." What we don't know at all we are not afraid of; as a sheep is happy, ignorant of the slaughter-house.

What we half-know scares us. Men used to be afraid of electricity, seeing it only in lightning; now they know it, and the motorman whistles as he regulates the power of ten thunderstorms.

All along, humanity has been walking up to bugaboos and finding out they were absurd.

Strange! Men have thought fear helped morality! They tortured, imprisoned, killed, to cure criminals. They beat children. They burned heretics. Gradually they saw their folly. They are learning that crime is essentially fear, the fear of the consequences of doing right, and that you cannot put out fire with kerosene; that is, you cannot cure the fear of doing right by the fear of punishment.

The Romans built a temple to fear. Fear has played a malign part in the history of religion. The most amazing creation of the human imagination is hell.

There are still those who are afraid to walk under a ladder, to carry a spade through the house, and to start on a journey on a Friday.

Business once was based on fear. Men thought the only way to get work done was by slaves, and by keeping them frightened. The capitalist and laborer still appealed to fear. But little by little the futility of it all is appearing.

Employers and employed are learning to appeal to the free cooperation of each other.

When men half-knew gods they trembled at them. *Timor fecit deos*— "fear made the gods." The race today fears and dreads God less because we are nearer Him than in the past.

Ignorance is the rust of the mind.

—RUST

CAREFUL AND COURAGEOUS

After reading the account of the exploits of a celebrated French aviator I come away with two words in my mind: Careful and Courageous.

In all his deeds of derring-do, in his appalling swoops and loops, now soaring to cold and dizzy heights, and again skimming close to earth and raking a troop-train with his machine-gun, landing once in enemy terrain and escaping by the skin of his teeth amidst a hail of bullets, he continually speaks of the precautions he takes, so that his carefulness was no less splendid than his courage.

If youth could only learn that! To be courageous, quick, daring, to strike hard and swiftly and fearlessly, and yet through it all to keep a clear head, to let the cool stream of prudence run beneath the high emprise!

For carefulness is not at all incompatible with bravery. In fact, it is the most fearless who are the most cautious.

The attack of the British in Zeebrugge, for instance, not only called for the maximum of fearlessness, but also for a nicety of calculation, a constant presence of mind, a perfection of team play.

It is not bravery alone that wins, but bravery plus intelligence. It is not prudence that is safest, but prudence plus courage and quick decision.

Often the most daring thing is the least dangerous. Often to hesitate and hedge is to incur the worst kind of risk.

Horsemen know this. Will S. Hart, who knows all there is to know about horses, told me that the secret of handling a vicious horse, a "man-killer," is to be unafraid. The animal seems to sense at once any element of fear in the man, and is quick to take advantage of it.

In business many a deal has been put through by decisiveness and firmness that would have been lost by faltering. Certain it is that those great captains of industry, men like Schwab or Jay Gould or Rockefeller, have exhibited quite as much daring in fateful crises as any general in battle. Yet behind their seeming recklessness was the shrewdest calculation.

Courage, in itself, is of not so great value. Animals have it, and stupid people, and the angry and frightened weakling. It may vent itself uselessly. It may be a fierce firing into the air. It is of not much use to be willing to shoot unless you know how to aim.

Careful and Courageous! These two words characterize the careers of such companions of danger as Quintus Fabius Maximus, the Duke of Wellington, Kitchener, Napoleon, Washington, Grant, and Funston.

Careful enough to leave no unnecessary preparations unmade; Courageous enough to seize the invaluable opportunity and strike when fortune beckons.

CATCH PHRASES

Volume 4

"Man shall not live by bread alone, but principally by catch-phrases," said Robert Louis Stevenson.

It is troublesome to think. The catch-phrase is ready-made thought. Most people much prefer it to their own.

This, of course, does not refer to you and me, but to the other fellows.

Multitudes live and die in sweet faith in a darling catch-phrase that is not true at all, or, what is worse, is half-true.

Most proverbs are but canned intellectual bromide. There are times, especially in life's crises, when the opposite of the old proverb, whatever it be that the wiseacres throw at you, is truer than the proverb itself.

Here are a few whiskered old flat ones I have met within in the last few days. Some of them were handed me by ladies; some I saw wandering down newspaper columns, some lay safely asleep in books.

"You can get nothing done without organization." The fact is that while, for a certain kind of efficiency organization, the institution is a good thing, there are certain other desirable results which organized effort absolutely prevents. For instance, there is a deal to be said on the other side, when it comes to the permanent value of the educational, the charitable, and the ecclesiastical institution.

"The Weaker Sex." A very dangerously truthful delusion. The man who gets the obsession that he is stronger than a woman usually comes to grief.

"To abate these crimes we need severer punishments." The idea that "the punishment should fit the crime," and that thereby crime will be estopped, belongs to the half-brute stage of civilization. Did you ever reflect that the root-difference between the New Testament and the Old consists in the abandonment of the punishment error? "An eye for an eye" was replaced by "turn the other cheek."

"Pure democracy consists in letting the people vote for every official and every measure." Quite the contrary. To overwhelm the citizen with responsibility for a mass of administrative detail is to throw, automatically, the government into the hands of the grafters. In an effective democracy the citizens vote for as few men and things as possible.

"We should all try to do good to others, to help and to uplift them." I think it was Thoreau who said that if he saw one coming with the intent to do him good he would take to his heels. The truth is that the most altruistic thing a man can do is to do justice himself, and to establish just conditions upon the earth. The merchant or manufacturer who supplies work for a hundred heads of families is greater in the Kingdom of Heaven than the rich man who gives charity to a thousand.

"Senators are all owned by Big Business; newspapers are all controlled from the business office; preachers are all afraid of the pew-renters; and all women are frail. There is no chance for an absolutely honest man. Graft, forwardness, deception, and pull gain all the prizes." The man who believes these things, the sooner he is nicely tucked under the sod the better for him and for us all. Senators, editors, priests, and women are mostly human, about as you and I. Most people would rather be decent and straight than not, simply because it is much more comfortable.

"To err is human." It is not to err that is peculiar to human beings. Beasts err also. That which is distinctly human is to realize that one has erred and to be sorry for it.

So it goes. Don't do your thinking in prepared pills. Don't eat intellectual canned goods exclusively.

CLEAN BUSINESS

Volume 5

Better than big business is clean business.

To an honest man the most satisfactory reflection after he has amassed his dollars is not that they are many but that they are all clean.

What constitutes clean business?

The answer is obvious enough,

but the obvious needs restating every once in a while.

A clean profit is one that has also made a profit for the other fellow.

This is the most fundamental moral axiom in business.

Any gain that arises from another's loss is dirty.

Any business whose prosperity depends upon damage to any other business is a menace to the general welfare.

That is why gambling, direct or indirect, is criminal, why lotteries are prohibited by law, and why even gambling slot-machine devices are not tolerated in civilized countries.

When a farmer sells a housekeeper a barrel of apples, when a milkman sells her a quart of milk, or the butcher a pound of steak, or the dry-goods man a yard of muslin, the housekeeper is benefited quite as much as those who get her money.

That is the type of honest, clean business, the kind that helps everybody and hurts nobody.

Of course as business becomes more complicated it grows more difficult to tell so clearly whether both sides are equally prospered. No principle is automatic. It requires sense, judgment, and conscience to keep clean; but it can be done, nevertheless, if one is determined to maintain his self-respect.

A man that makes a habit, every deal he goes into, of asking himself, "What is there in it for the other fellow?" and who refuses to enter into any transaction where his own gain will mean disaster to someone else, cannot go far wrong.

And no matter how many memorial churches he builds, nor how much he gives to charity, or how many monuments he erects in his native town, any man who has made his money by ruining other people is not entitled to be called decent.

A factory where many workmen are given employment, paid living wages, and where health and life are conserved, is doing more real good in the world than ten eleemosynary* institutions.

The only really charitable dollar is the clean dollar.

And the nasty dollar, wrung from wronged workmen or gotten by unfair methods from competitors, is never nastier than when it pretends to serve the Lord by being given to the poor, to education, or to religion. In the long run all such dollars tend to corrupt and disrupt society.

Of all vile money, that which is the most unspeakably vile is the money spent for war; for war is conceived by the blundering ignorance and selfishness of rulers, is fanned to flame by the very lowest passions of humanity, and prostitutes the highest ideal of men—zeal for the common good—to the business of killing human beings and destroying the results of their collective work.

Anger is self-esteem on fire. —ANGER

*supported by charity

COCK-SURENESS

It is as bad to be too cock-sure of things as it is to be a doubter. Somewhere between these two extremes you want to build your house.

The great point is, to be sure enough of a thing, so as to be able to use it, to live by it, to take it as a rule of conduct or a basis of morals, and at the same time to admit that you may be mistaken, and therefore, to be open to conviction.

There are many truths good enough to work with in the world, that cannot be declared absolutely indubitable. In fact the most vital and necessary truths are precisely the ones that are essentially dubitable. You must eat, and you don't know the food is not poison; you must sleep, yet you don't know an earthquake will not tumble your house down on you; you must love, and you never know absolutely, you can only believe, that love is returned; you must obey God, and live for an immortal life, yet no man has seen God, at any time, and none has returned from the shades beyond the grave. The higher, nobler, and more worthy a man's life, the more it is woven of questionable, debatable material.

This we find out when we grow old. When we are young we are cock-sure. "Every new idea," says Castelar, "tends to make itself absolute, tends to cancel all limits, to break over all opposition to believe itself to be the only idea fit to live in the universe, and sufficient to solve all problems."

COLUMBUS

America lies beyond. Nothing is final!

So many people give up. If they would go on they would discover America.

That little company on the Pinta, the Nina, and the Santa Maria are a good type of us all. They were afraid. All about them was the dreadful unknown. Imagination had peopled the sea with monsters. They were sailing where man had never sailed before, which calls for the last reserves of courage. They wanted to turn back. They threatened mutiny. Only the iron-willed Columbus said, "Sail on!"

So we venture on into tomorrow,

an uncharted water. We know not what we shall find. The ghosts of our fears and fancies threaten us. We shrink from the future. We would quit, turn back. We are like the sailors. But let me rather be like Columbus.

For America lies beyond.

Nothing is final.

Have you lost your money? Has your business failed? Is poverty staring you in the face? You know not which way to turn. You say you are "up against it." You sit and brood. Despair is your companion.

Go on! Tomorrow lies before you. Who knows what is there? Perhaps the land of success is just beyond the horizon and tomorrow's sun will reveal it, palm-fringed and glistening.

You have lost your position. You have lost your love. Disgrace has fallen upon you. Disease has attacked you. Friends have deserted you. Or some other calamity shadows you.

Go on! Life is not a fixed point. Life is a stream, ever flowing. It is a moving picture continually unfolding. It is a strange tale; there will be another chapter after this. Let us see what is in it.

Thank God! no man knows the future. Let our curiosity keep up our spirit. Life is an unending adventure.

America lies beyond.

Nothing is final.

Life is a puzzle. But every puzzle has a solution. To high hearts and undaunted minds there is always hope.

Come! Faces toward the future! Pull the belt a little tighter! Speak cheer one to another! Whatever has happened to us or in us, whatever outward evil or inward weakness, we are not cattle, nor rabbits; we are souls, a little fragment each of us of the Almighty God; no one can make us despair except ourself.

If I fall I shall rise again. The fates may be very strong, but they cannot make me afraid.

My soul is a Columbus; and not watery wastes, nor strange sounds, nor glooming mysteries, nor bludgeoning facts, not heaven nor hell shall send me back, nor make me cry "Enough!"

America lies beyond.

Nothing is final.

We are so dazzled by ideals that we cannot see the supreme privilege of freedom is freedom to do wrong. . . . Virtue is of account only in one who might have chosen vice.

—THE RIGHT TO MAKE ONE'S OWN MISTAKES

THE COMEBACK

I find that the way I am treated in any company depends upon the state of mind I bring into it.

If I enter a circle of men and women whom I take to be superior to me, I am likely to be snubbed. If I impute to them the feeling that I am inferior I will not fail to be inferior.

If I am self-confident I awaken confidence.

If I cringe I make others want to step on me.

If I am cheerful, cheerfulness is handed me by others.

If I am grouchy and snappy, they will bite me.

People go at me about the way I go at them.

There is a law in physics to the effect that action is equal to reaction. The ball rebounds from the wall with precisely the force with which it was thrown against the wall.

And if I approach a man with politeness I usually receive politeness.

I get from this world a smile for a smile, a kick for a kick, love for love, and hate for hate.

Of course there are exceptions to this rule. But if there were no rule there would be no exceptions.

And the difference between the man who knows how to play a game and wins regularly—any game, including poker and the game of life—and the man who steadily loses is that the wise man sticks to the rules and the law of averages, and the fool "has a hunch" and stakes his all on the exceptions.

A good definition of a fool is one who thinks that this time doesn't count.

My tablets, therefore! Meet it is I set it down that I am getting what is coming to me.

This is a world of law. Chance is to be found only in the dictionary. In the bright lexicon of fact there's no such word.

If I am petulant, unrestful, irritable, unsatisfied, wretched, and bored—I know the crop, and might have expected the harvest when I sowed that seed of self-indulgence, lack of will, moral cowardice, and general selfishness.

If I am lonely, it was I who drove hearts away.

If I am bitter, it was I who skimped the sugar-bowl.

If I am persecuted, it was I who brought it on by my cantankerousness.

The loving are beloved.

The generous are helped.

The considerate are considered.

The bully by and by is bullied, the smasher smashed.

And the end of the hog is the slaughter-house.

There are no victims of fate. The hero always rises above tragedy. The noble soul is never more serene than when all creation thinks it has drowned him.

CONFUSION

Volume 8

Every evil is but confusion.

What strikes you when talking with a criminal is his jumbled vision. He has lost all sense of proportion. He imagines the most absurd things to be worthwhile.

Alcohol is the chief of crime-breeders because it befogs the mind.

The best man is the man who sees most clearly.

Ignorance is not absence of knowledge. The lout knows as much as the savant; only his facts are pell-mell, his information is litter. Having no mental order, he has no force. The ignorant mind is not a blank, it is a dump-heap.

Disease is confusion. Good health is the harmony of all one's organs. Pain is physical mutiny, riot, and conflagration among the cells. When the liver, pancreas, stomach, nerves, and the rest keep step, and march along sweetly by companies to the music of cheerful thoughts, you are well; you are ill when they break ranks and become a mob.

Insanity is mental confusion.

Morbidity, despair, self-pity, and all the doltish doldrums of the mind are indications of undisciplined thought.

What we call sin is but confusion of desires. The commanding captains—wisdom, will, and principle—have abdicated. The soldiers are given over to looting.

Love is order. It is a sort of superwisdom, a divine wisdom, feeling what the intelligence cannot reach.

Love correlates, adjusts all things. It diagnoses accurately.

It sees far ahead, even to eternity. It is not blinded by the present. It is not hampered and deceived by experience.

Love estimates truly, sees relative values, apprehends essentials.

Jealousy, hate, estrangement, are blind. They stumble. They do not see facts, but butt their heads against them, for they grope in the dark. Success, in a real sense, never comes save as the result of seeing clearly what we want.

If you are confused, do nothing.

Wait until the storms blow over.

Goodness is clarity of heart. Wisdom is clarity of mind. Happiness is clarity of soul.

Faith, hope, and clarity, these three—but the greatest of these is clarity.

THE COWARDICE OF PESSIMISM

Volume 1

Pessimism is the fine name for cowardice, vulgarity, self-pity, and failure.

Pessimists are all cowards, in that realm where cowardice is most fatal, that is to say, in the region of spiritual and moral potencies. They are afraid of kindness, for they may not be thanked, afraid of goodness on account of the moral effort involved, afraid of justice, sorrow, and death, which are the ennobling facts of life.

They are vulgar, because it is an unvarying trait of the vulgar mind to find fault rather than to commend.

They are victims of that most disgusting disease of the soul, self-pity, for they always assume superiority to that world of which they complain, and regard themselves as superfine souls ill-used.

They are egotists, for their assumed standard of excellence is self, not things and men as they are.

They are failures, for, as Carl Hilty says, "pessimists are those who have somehow fallen short and are incapable of struggling with courage for the highest things of life, and of gaining them by the power and endurance necessary."

CREATURE OR CREATOR

Volume 4

Are you Creature or Creator? Says Ernest Crosby:

"Where are the cowards who bow down to environment—

"Who think they are made of what they eat?

"I am not wax. I am energy.

"I have my ideas to work out, and the universe is given me for raw material.

"I am a vortex launched in chaos to suck it into shape."

It all depends upon your point of view. You can be either clay or potter, the ball or the pitcher, a thing or a god.

Why do you talk of being the victim of circumstances? You can just as well be the master of circumstances.

I am no puppet of fate. I am secretly in partnership with fate.

Whatever else He may be, God is a spirit. And I am also a spirit.

He is not an image of stone. Neither am I a mere organism of flesh.

He leads the stars, informs the lily, guides the wayward river, moulds the raindrop, turns on the aurora, and drives the chariot of the sun.

I, who am His kin, am also no clod.

I find a way. I create opportunity. I yoke the winds to my sails and the stream to my cylinders.

I speak to bricks and they fall in by platoons and become my walls.

I gesture to electricity, and it lights my house, draws my roaring express-train, and carries my words in a flash across continents and under oceans.

I can also make tears and laughter. I can darken hearts with pain and light them with joy.

I can discourage the eager boy and soil the clean soul of the girl. I can sow doubt, discord, discontent. I can be as efficient in evil as the devil.

I have no excuse. If I have got drunk it was I who swallowed the stuff. I must pay the debts of my madness.

If I have failed, seek no further. It is I who am to blame. For there is to me no failure anywhere in the world that counts, except the failure within my soul.

No man, no woman can defile me. The soul's next is never fouled save by itself.

And if I have succeeded, give me the credit and not another, nor luck, nor happenings.

For success is spiritual somewhat. Even when it comes to the inward failure he cannot hold it. It falls from his hands.

I take my reward. I take my punishment. Both are mine.

I am no horse. No one rides me and pulls my bridle. I am the rider.

I can go to hell if I want to. I can go to heaven if I prefer.

I am a free spirit. All around me and within me flows the Universal Spirit. He is Creator. So am I. We work together.

If I have poise and peace and prosperity it is due to us, to our creative partnership.

I am no Creature. I am co-Creator.

Love excuses everything —among men.
Passion excuses everything—among brutes.
—THOUGHTS ON LOVE

DAD

Dear Dad: I am writing this to you, though you have been dead thirty years.

From your seat in the Place Beyond I hope you can see these lines. I feel I must say some things to you, things I didn't know when I was a boy in your house, and things I was too stupid to say.

It's only now, after passing through the long, hard school of years, only now, when my own hair is gray, that I understand how you felt.

I must have been a bitter trial to you. I was such an ass. I believed my own petty wisdom, and I know now how ridiculous it was, compared to that calm, ripe, wholesome wisdom of yours.

Most of all, I want to confess my worst sin against you. It was the feeling I had that you "did not understand."

When I look back over it now, I know that you did understand. You understood me better than I did myself. Your wisdom flowed around mine like the ocean around an island.

And how patient you were with me! How full of long-suffering, and kindness!

And how pathetic,* it now comes home to me, were your efforts to get close to me, to win my confidence, to be my pal!

I wouldn't let you. I couldn't. What was it held me aloof? I don't know. But it is tragic—that wall that rises between a boy and his father, and their frantic attempts to see through it and climb over it.

I wish you were here now, across the table from me, just for an hour, so that I could tell you how there's no wall anymore; I understand you now, Dad, and, God! how I love you, and wish I could go back and be your boy again.

I know now how I could make you happy every day. I know how you felt.

Well, it won't be long, Dad, till I am over, and I believe you'll be the first one to take me by the hand and help me up the further slope.

And I'll put in the first thousand years or so making you realize that not one pang or yearning you spent on me was wasted.

It took a good many years for this prodigal son—and all sons are in a measure prodigal—to come to himself, but I've come, I see it all now.

I know that the richest, most priceless thing on earth, and the thing least understood, is that mighty love and tenderness and craving to help which a father feels toward his boy.

*sad

For I have a boy of my own.

And it is he that makes me want to go back to you, and get down on my knees to you.

Up there somewhere in the silence, hear me, Dad, and believe me.

DEPENDENCE

Man is essentially a dependent creature. He is like certain sea-beings, such as the pantecrinis caput medusæ, which cannot live, though they be animals, without attaching themselves to some rock or shell.

When you examine any human greatness, you will always find it consists in a human spirit finding some cause or principle or person and giving himself up to it. There is no heroism that is not self-surrender.

The good mother is one who is tied to her children. A man's passions never become noble until they are chained to the one woman he has chosen. It is this sense of servitude, of bondage, of obedience to another in our innermost will and feeling, that lends honor and stature to our commonest human relations. Jesus was never taller than when he called himself "Servant of all." And it was said of Him, "It behooved the captain of our salvation to learn obedience."

Freedom is only a superficial and a relative term; it can only mean renouncing a lower master for a higher one.

Those who are independent of every government are properly called pirates and bandits, and are hunted down by all nations as enemies of mankind.

Those who seek to be entirely independent, to do as they please, to be their own master, become speedily slaves to the worst of masters, their own appetites.

The beauty of a worthy master is that he sets us free. Only as we find that to which we can look up and reverence, and as we find that which is reverencing, do we escape from the irritating slavery of self. "If the Son shall make you free, ye shall be free indeed."

If you ask what I gain by being good, by doing what is just and fair, I answer: I gain my own self-respect.

—THE WAY OUT

DESPAIR

"Kindly give me your advice what I should do," writes a correspondent. "When I came to America I was about ten years old, my parents dead. I was not able to go to school, and now that I am older I find out that life is not worth anything to me without education. After all these wasted years I am trying to study, but it seems to me I haven't any brain to study. I am so very tired of the struggle that I have decided to end my life, and I am sure you will agree with me. You know very well a person without education is not worth anything. It is not my fault, for I was compelled to go to work and struggle till this very day. I was born on Friday the 13th."

I give this letter exactly as it is written, with a few verbal corrections. It presents a very real problem.

It is the problem of despair, and is peculiarly difficult and distressing.

Despair is a collapse of the ego, a paralysis of the will, a failure of the vital force. It is as hard to tell a victim of despair what to do as it is for a physician to prescribe for a patient whose heart has given out.

Suicide presupposes insanity, for the last instinct of the mind is the desire to live.

All we can do is to recognize the approaches to despair, take them in time, and endeavor to correct them. These approaches are as follows:

1. Fear. Any kind of fear strikes at the center of life, tends to dissolve the moral force and to derange the reason. All forms of fear, including worry, apprehension, superstition (such as indicated in the above letter by the reference to Friday the 13th), should be vigorously combated. Courage is the universal cure of souls.

2. Self contempt. Resist all thoughts that make you despise yourself. Assert yourself; assert your right to live, to succeed, to be happy. Self-pity is the peculiar poison of the devil. Never give way to it. Don't think failure. Fight the good fight to the last ditch.

3. Gloomy and morbid fancies. When these come to you shake them off, get out, and get busy. Don't read pessimistic books. Don't listen to doleful people. Resist the shadows. Keep in the sunlight.

4. Depressing surroundings. Get away from them. To do so may imply losing money, or station in life, or friends, but better lose these than life itself. Go where there is cheer and health and brightness, if it costs you all you own in the world.

5. Words. Don't talk failure, gloom, disappointment, or darkness.

Words react upon you. Talk hope, success, victory. Affirm God. Affirm you own soul. Affirm joy. Talk energy, not weakness.

Every human being has to fight more or less against the forces of disintegration within him. Despair is the enemy of all mankind. It is the devil's other name. Let us struggle against it day and night.

We are all a little crazy; let us cheer one another up as best we can.

As the Spaniards say:

"De medico, poeta y loco
Todos tenemos un poco."

Everybody has in him a bit of the physician, the poet, and the madman.

THE DESTRUCTION OF PLEASURE

Volume 2

The aim of all culture is to maintain and develop the capacity for pleasure. The advantage of an education, of acquiring superior taste, and of getting away from the sensual and over into the intellectual life, is that one finds satisfactions that are more enduring.

Nobody denies that there is pleasure in eating and drinking. The trouble with these delightful exercises is that they are limited. No matter how refined and varied a career of material enjoyment may be, after awhile it grows stale.

Most short-sighted human beings imagine that if they had riches they could be happy, because they would be able to increase the number of their physical sensations. Their notion of heaven on earth is to dine sumptuously, to ride in expensive automobiles, to have plenty of servants, to bedizen their bodies with rare clothes, to load their fingers with diamonds and their skins with perfumes.

One only needs, however, to go and visit the supposed fortunate ones who possess all these longed-for luxuries to be disabused of the idea that such things can make happiness. You will find them, as a rule, bored, petulant, and vulgar.

Only those can resist the inevitable destructiveness of wealth who have been carefully trained and have learned to appreciate simplicity—to dress modestly, to eat sparingly, to speak restrainedly, and to conduct themselves unobtrusively.

There are those who have long been accustomed to riches who thus manage to attain greatness in spite of them, and these excite our admiration because they are rare.

But the goal is quite as easily attained by the poor as by the rich.

Sensual gratification destroys the joy of both rich and poor; of the former because they have a superfluity of material satisfactions, of the latter because they crave them.

Shelly says, in his Defense of Poetry: "The end of social corruption is to destroy the sensibility to pleasure. It begins by the imagination and intellect as the core, and distributes itself thence as a paralyzing venom into the affections and the very appetites, until all become a torpid mass in which hardly sense survives."

The Dhammapada

Volume 8

More people delight in proverbs than one would suppose. You will be surprised to find how many persons copy in their commonplace book, or hang upon their wall by the mirror or over the desk, certain pithy apothegms that strike their fancy.

For their benefit let me here give some sayings that are found in the Dhammapada, or Verses of Teaching. They represent pretty faithfully the doctrine of Buddha, but their high ethical value will be appreciated by the West.

It may be well for us to chew these Oriental bits of wisdom thoughtfully, and we may, so doing, realize what has been said of them, "a little thereof saves from much sorrow."

According to Buddha, the sources of sorrow are three: craving, ill-will (or hate), and delusion (or ignorance).

As rain gets into an ill-thatched house, so craving gets into an ill-trained mind.

If a man hates, "suffering follows him close, as the wheel follows the hoof of the beast that draws the cart."

"If a man talks much about the truth, but acts not in accordance with it, he is but little better than the cowherd who counts the cattle of others." What more striking picture have you seen than this, of the dilettante who is as one that counts other people's cattle?

"The man who is vigilant over himself makes to himself an island that no flood can overwhelm."

"The one who has attained self-mastery has ascended the tower of wisdom, whence he looks down, free from sorrow, upon the sorrow-laden race of mankind."

Those who attain the secret of

life, according to Buddha, do not attain it by knowledge, but by what is called the awakening. Coming from ignorance to wisdom is like waking from sleep and dreams to reality.

"A guarded mind brings happiness."

"The mind is seated in the hollow of the heart." Perhaps this means that there is no real intelligent perception without love.

"To the mind accustomed to delusion the truth is unpleasant and fearsome, even as a fish quivers and throbs when thrown up out of the water on the land."

The influence of one's mind is compared to the fragrance of flowers. "The fragrance of flowers, of sandal, or incense, or jasmine, is not wafted against the wind; but the fragrance of wisdom is wafted against the wind."

"If on a journey you can find no one better than nor equal to yourself, then go your way alone. A fool is no company."

"Riches are mine, thinks the fool. But a man that does not know himself, much less can he know riches."

"Though a fool meet wise men and hear wisdom his whole life long, yet he remains ignorant of the truth, as a spoon of the flavor of soup."

"Look upon him who makes you see your defects as upon one who points you out a treasure."

"Be it village or forest, on land or sea, where the noble mind dwells is the place to be."

The teaching of the Buddha, says Silacara, is summed up in a famous stanza as simply that "everything in the world comes into existence from some cause, and with the ceasing of that cause the thing ceases." The hearing of this stanza was the occasion of the conversion of one of the Buddha's most famous disciples. Apparently simple, almost to the point of banality, as this statement is, yet the unreserved acceptance of its truth leads to what is called the Truth Supreme, which is that "everything that exists is conditioned and dependent."

DOING CLEARS THE MIND

Volume 1

Doing clears the mind. Physical activity has a peculiar luminous effect upon the judgment. The soundest views of life come not from the pulpit or the professional chair, but from the workshop. To saw a plank or nail down a shingle, to lay a stone square or paint a house evenly, to run a locomotive or raise a good crop of corn, somehow reacts upon the intelligence, reaching the very inward essential cell of wisdom; provided always the worker is brave, not afraid of his own conclusions, and does not hand his thinking over to some guesser with a large bluff. Doing makes religion. All the religion that is of any account is what we thresh out with our own hands, suffer out with our own hearts, and find out with our own visions. Doing creates faith. Doubt comes from Sundays, and other idle hours. The only people who believe the Ten Commandments are those who do them. Those who believe the world is growing better are they that are trying to make it grow better. Doing brings joy. The sweetest of joys is the joy of accomplishment. Make love and you will feel love. Quit making love and you will doubt love. Be kind, steadily and persistently, and you will believe in kindness. Be unclean and you will soon sneer at anybody's claim to virtue. Be mean and you will cease to believe there is any goodness in the world.

So a man has his own destiny, his own creed, his own internal peace, his own nobility in his hands—literally in his *hands*. For all the worthwhile wisdom of goodness you have in your head and heart was soaked up from your hands.

DUMB DANGER

Volume 5

I have said that business that is dumb* is dangerous. I will go further. It is dangerous because it is dumb.

When there is power it must exert itself in some way. In man the normal way is through art—letters, painting, sculpture, music.

That is why art is the great civilizer. It furnishes an outlet for human energy, and such an outlet, such a mode of expression, as conserves, develops, idealizes, and improves the quality of that energy.

Without art, energy manifests itself destructively, or at least coarsely.

The profane person uses oaths because he cannot express his feelings in proper words. If he knew the art of speech he wouldn't swear.

What a man can utter in a word a dumb animal can utter only by biting, howling, butting, rending.

All power that is dumb is dangerous.

*mute

Let us take, for instance, a great public-utility corporation, serving millions of people, a prime necessity of communal life. It goes along for years in prosperity, and then, when it approaches the legislature for a favor, or when in some crisis it finds itself in a dispute where it needs the support of public opinion, it is suddenly made aware that there exists toward it among the people a dull hostility.

Its directors get together and are apt to exclaim against the ingratitude of people, and to talk of envy, jealousy, socialism, and the hate toward wealth.

It would do these directors good if they could be made to see what is the matter. The matter is that they have been dumb.

A persistent campaign of advertising would have changed all that hostility to friendship.

If you want me to feel friendly toward you, you must talk to me.

Human nature is human nature. If a man in a village never speaks he will be suspected of all manner of crimes.

A non-advertising corporation is to a state or nation what this dumb man is to the village. Things may go well with it until it needs public cooperation and help; then it discovers that it has foolishly alienated the people.

The more power a man or an organization of men has, the more it needs advertising as a matter of self-preservation.

DUTY

Volume 8

The very best kind of man and the most useful to his fellows is the man who does what he ought to do.

There is but one cowardice, it is not doing one's duty. There is but one failure, the failure to discharge an obligation. There is but one sin, not doing what we ought.

The biggest word in the language is *ought*. The man who keeps it bright within him, always visible and always revered, is a real man.

There is so much of the superfluous among us, so much glory in affairs that are none of our business, so much success that is essential treachery, and so much goodness that is but interesting meanness.

It is better to keep your word than to speak pleasantly.

It is better to tell the truth than to lie entertainingly.

It is better to be loyal than to be affectionate.

It is better honestly to earn the wages paid you than to have grand ideas on the labor problem.

It is better to earn your living and take yourself off other people's backs than to be a saint or a genius.

It is better for you, if you are an employer, to give your workers fair wages, and a little more, to treat them with consideration, and to recognize them as human beings than to wring money from them to give to charity.

It is better to be honest toward women than attractive.

It is better for a woman to deceive no man than to win one.

It is better to pay your debts than to give to the poor.

It is better to have a little efficiency than a lot of knowledge.

It is better to do one good act than to speak many good words.

One earned dollar is worth more to you than a thousand given you.

"There are," said Elizabeth Inchbald, "persons who love to do everything good but that which their immediate duty requires. There are servants that will serve everyone more cheerfully than their own masters; there are men who will distribute money liberally to all except their creditors, and there are wives who will love all mankind better than their husbands. We have acts of generosity, self-denial, and honesty where smaller pains would constitute greater virtues."

Duty is the egg of all goodness.

It is the primordial protoplasm from which all organized excellences develop.

Without it religion is hypocrisy, love is poison, activity useless, kindness cruelty, and every good quality as a red apple full of wormy meat.

THE DUTY OF THE RICH

It is the duty of the rich to live as simply as possible.

The rich are a privileged class. Along with every privilege comes a responsibility. And the responsibility that rests upon wealthy people is to do by choice and strength what poor people have to do by necessity and weakness, to wit: to deny themselves.

Poverty is not a blessing. It is a curse. It tends to crush out the finer elements of character, to smother all expression of culture under the fierce need of getting bread and butter.

Therefore, it is right that the general standard of living should rise.

There can be no decent development of life where one must work ten hours a day at such labor as leaves him no time for leisure, recreation, and improvement.

But when the standard of living rises to the point where people are unhappy without luxuries and extravagances, it is bad.

It is the constant sight of the display made by the rich that fosters discontent among the poor, and is the ruination of the middle class.

There is something coarse about the woman who can spend thousands of dollars upon expensive furs, parade at the theatre box with diamonds costing a fortune, and quench her thirst with liquid that sells at ten dollars a short quart. I am no judge to say she is wicked. But she certainly has a common, vulgar soul if she can do this, knowing that multitudes of her sister women are spent and troubled by the pressure of real want.

I don't know what rich people ought to do with their money, and am not in a position where the problem faces me personally. Socialism, anarchism, nationalism, communism do not convince me that they would surely cure the ills of society, though I am willing to try any of them if the rest of you so wish. But I do think that it is time that vulgar extravagance and idleness of upper tendom ceased to flaunt themselves. If a man wants to do nothing but buy champagne, play polo, sail in a private yacht, live in a ducal mansion, and own seventeen automobiles, I am in favor of his doing it; this is a free country, and I like once in a while to take a little fling myself of which the sewing-circle might not approve. But self-indulgence at least ought to have the decency to crawl off and hide.

The influence of displaying in the Sunday newspapers, in magazines, and in novels, the antics of the idle set, their waste and their perversion, tends to vulgarize the whole people.

There is some respectable authority for the statement that the rich man will have a hard time squeezing into the kingdom of heaven; but at least he might give the poor on this earth a chance to get in, and not ruin them by dangling his vulgar self-pamperings forever before their eyes.

If you trust a friend, trust him unto death. Of course you may be deceived in him. But better be humiliated by betrayal than be incapable of perfect faith.

—FEAR OF GREATNESS

EFFICIENCY

Make good! Don't explain! Do the thing you are expected to do! Don't waste time in giving reasons why you didn't, or couldn't, or wouldn't, or shouldn't!

If I hire you to cook for me I expect my chops and baked potatoes on time, done to a turn and appetizing; I am not interested in the butcher's mistake, nor the stove's defect, nor in the misery in your left arm. I want food, not explanations. You can't eat explanations.

If I hire you to take care of my automobile, or factory, or shirtwaist counter, I do not want to hear why things are half-done; I want results.

So also if you come to me and hire me to do a job of writing by the fifteenth of the month, you do not want me to show up on that day with a moving-picture story describing how I couldn't do what I was paid for. You want the writing, and you want it first class, all wool and a yard wide.

This is cold, cruel, heartless talk. It is—to all second-raters and shirkers. But to real men it is a joy and gladness. They rejoice to make good themselves, they expect others to make good, and they like to hear preached the gospel of making good.

Mr. Yust, the Rochester librarian, in his report some time ago, spoke of the Parable of the Talents, in which we are told of the "three servants who had received talents, five, two, and one, respectively. On the Master's return they all rendered account of their stewardship. The first two had doubled their capital. Each of them said so in fourteen words, and their work was pronounced, 'Well done, good and faithful servant.' Servant number three had accomplished absolutely nothing, but he made a full report in forty-two words, three times as long as the other reports."

There you have it. The less you do the more you explain.

EFFICIENCY!

Learn that word by heart. Get to saying it in your sleep.

Of all the joys on this terrestrial sphere, there is none quite so soul-satisfying and so one-hundred-per-centish as MAKING GOOD.

Do your work a little better than anyone else could do it. That is the margin of success.

Making good needs no footnotes.

Failure requires forty-two words.

Any gain that arises from another's loss is dirty.

—CLEAN BUSINESS

THE ENEMY

Whoever you are there's somebody that doesn't like you.

The one constant figure on life's stage is the enemy. He's always there, sitting grim and silent, or busy with hostility.

"Be thou as pure as ice, as chaste as snow, thou shalt not escape calumny."

Gentle maiden, as good as fair, with a heart warm and kind to all God's creatures, anxious to spread happiness as May to spread flowers, it seems incredible, but there is someone to whom your presence is offense, and to whom your surcease would be pleasing!

In the chemistry of souls this repellency is most curious, but undeniable. No human force ever comes into the world without its opposite. Every positive has its negative. In every love is a little spot of hate. Heaven and hell, in their deeper significance, touch every human heart.

Cæsar had his Brutus, Socrates his Meletus, and Jesus the envious Pharisees.

When I read any book that pleases me, human Dickens or quiet Wordsworth, the exquisitely tooled woodcraft of Vernon Lee or the smashing liveliness of Conan Doyle, it often comes to me—somebody doesn't like this.

Queer, isn't it? Sinister and strange, but true. Little dove, the hawk soars stilly watching; little fly, the spider swings ready in his web; little doe, the cougar crouches behind the bush; little soul, among the gods walks one who looks darkly at you.

And the higher you climb, the brighter you write your name upon fame's scroll, the louder your applause and the more signal your triumph, the surer there will be, somewhere muffled in the cheering crowd, the sombre figure of some "Mordecai sitting at the king's gate."

Is not America a beloved country? There are those who loathe it unreservedly. Is not President Wilson a fine figure among statesmen? There are many who would rejoice at his downfall, who watch eagerly to find his mistakes and herald them.

In a way the strength of the enemy is a reliable measure of one's success. The more you amount to, the sharper the hisses. Many a man has been elected to Congress by his enemies, and many a writer has been hounded to fame.

The best way to meet the enemy is to let him see that you do not think it worthwhile to fight him. Nothing so enrages malice as to discover that you don't mind. Nothing so disarms attack as for you to go about your business as usual. Such defense is more effective than blows; kindness is the most exasperating vengeance.

When in doubt, say nothing. Your enemy can answer everything you can possibly say, can retaliate against everything you can possibly do, except one thing. That is silence.

THE ETHICS OF CONTROVERSY

Everything is disputable. I am willing to entertain arguments in support of any proposition whatsoever.

If you want to defend theft, mayhem, adultery, or murder, state your case, bring on your reasons; for in endeavoring to prove an indefensible thing you discover for yourself how foolish is your thesis.

But it is essential to any controversy, if it is to be of any use, first, that the issue be clearly understood by both sides.

Most contentions amount merely to a difference of definition. Agree, therefore, exactly upon what it is you are discussing. If possible, set down your statements in writing.

Most argument is a wandering from the subject, a confusion of the question, an increasing divergence from the point. Stick to the matter in hand.

When your adversary brings in subjects not relevant, do not attempt to answer them. Ignore them, lest you both go astray and drift into empty vituperation.*

For instance, President Wilson, in the *Lusitania* incident, called Germany's attention to the fact that her submarines had destroyed a merchant ship upon the high seas, the whole point being that this had been done without challenge or search and without giving non-combatant citizens of a neutral country a chance for their lives. Germany's reply discussed points that had no bearing upon this issue, such as various acts of England. Mr. Wilson, in his reply, wisely refused to discuss these irrelevant things, an example of intelligent controversy.

Keep cool. The worse your case, the louder your voice.

Be courteous. Avoid epithets. Do not use language calculated to anger or offend your opponent. Such terms weaken the strength of your position.

A controversy is a conflict of reasons, not of passions. The more

*argument

heat the less sense.

Keep down your ego. Do not boast. Do not emphasize what you think, what you believe, and what you feel; but try to put forth such statements as will induce your opponent to think, believe, and feel rationally.

Wait. Give your adversary all the time he wants to vent his views. Let him talk himself out. Wait your turn, and begin only when he is through.

Agree with him as far as you can. Give due weight, and a little more, to his opinions. It was the art of Socrates, the greatest of controversialists, to let a man run the length of his rope; that is, to talk until he had himself seen the absurdity of his contention.

Most men argue simply to air their convictions. Give them room. Often when they have fully exhausted their notions they will come gently back to where you want them. They are best convinced when they convince themselves.

Avoid tricks, catches, and the like. Do not take advantage of your opponent's slip of the tongue. Let him have the impression that you are treating him fairly.

Do not get into any discussion unless you can make it a sincere effort to discover the truth, and not to overcome, out-talk, or humiliate your opponent.

Do not discuss at all with one who has his mind made up beforehand. It is usually profitless to argue upon religion, because as a rule men's opinions here are reached not by reason but by feeling or by custom. Nothing is more interesting and profitable, however, than to discuss religion with an open-minded person, yet such a one is a very rare bird.

If you meet a man full of egotism or prejudices, do not argue with him. Let him have his say, agree with him as you can, and for the rest—smile.

Controversy may be made a most friendly and helpful exercise, if it be undertaken by two well-tempered and courteous minds.

Vain contention, on the contrary, is of no use except to deepen enmity.

Controversy is a game for strong minds; contention is a game for the weak and undisciplined.

Freedom, then, does not signify the absence of restraint . . . . Freedom signifies simply that you shall not put your restraints upon me.

—LIBERTY

EVERY DAY

Every day!

In those two words lies the secret of all attainment.

It's not what we do once, with all our hearts, and with every splendid ounce of strength, that counts, so much as the things we've been doing every day, whether we felt like it or not.

Every day! Therein is mastery. The marvelous, velvet, utterly exquisite beauty of such piano-playing as Paderewski's, or such violin performance as Maud Powell's—it looks spontaneous, but it is the result of many a hateful day's laborious routine.

Every day! That is the road to perfection. The speaker who can hold and charm an audience, the debater quick and ready and not to be confused, the baseball player, the woman always socially at ease—everybody, in fact, that can do anything well owes that poise and finish to the slow efforts of every day.

No matter how gifted an actor, how naturally endowed, he cannot be a master without infinite practise.

Young people do not realize the tremendous cumulative power that lies in time. Take ten years. Say you are twenty. By the time you are thirty what enormous efficiency you might build up if you would only use every day a certain amount of time.

Almost everybody wastes enough hours in ten years to get a doctor's degree in any university.

In ten years you might be speaking and reading fluently Spanish or French or Japanese; you might be an authority upon geology, botany, chemistry, English literature, history, or whatever fits your ambition, if you would only be faithful every day.

Every day! The universe is constructed on routine. The sun rises every day, the stars revolve, the seasons come and go by schedule, your heart beats, and your lungs fill and empty as regularly as the clock ticks. Every generation of men or of animals is the result of numberless preceding generations. Over and over again Nature tries her hand, and her matchless perfection is only the stored-up treasure of endless practise.

And in character every day means even more than anywhere else. The most honest man is the man who has been honest every day; the most virtuous woman is she who has behind her present virtue the inertia of a whole life full of virtuous thought and deed; the happiest person is the one who has long practised being happy, and that soul is coolest and surest in a crisis who every day has schooled himself in self-mastery.

No force is so great in any man as the stored-up power of what he has been doing every day.

EXPERIMENTS IN DEFINITION

—— *Volume 5*

God. The eternal spirit of goodness and justice that dominates all events and pervades all things.

Law. The right of way.

Righteousness. That course of conduct that invariably and in the long run produces happiness.

Wisdom. Adjusting one's self to law.

Fool. One who expects happiness in violation of law.

Courage. Placing adherence to what is true and right above personal pleasure or safety or life itself.

Faith. Confidence in the eternal cosmic laws of goodness, that they are stronger than anything evil, and that it pays to commit one's self wholly to them.

Passion. Feeling that rises to the point of dominance.

Purity. The elimination of selfishness from passion.

Pride. The morbid overestimate of self; moral auto-infection.

Charity. Love operating upon judgment.

Humility. The normal attitude of a healthy mind toward itself.

Sympathy. Feeling another's suffering or pleasure as if it were one's own.

Chastity. The intelligent choice of and preference for the finer over the coarser pleasures of love.

Forgiveness. The elimination of all sense of offense at another's action toward us.

Honor. A high sense of what is right and wrong, held in regard to one's own judgment and without regard to the opinions of others.

Love. The inspirational effect of one personality upon another.

Religion. The personal influence of God and of the Godlike in human beings.

Temperance. Self-control, the last and greatest of all virtues, the regulating virtue, producing poise and order in one's life.

Repentance. Sorrow over wrong of which we have been guilty.

Tolerance. Hospitality of opinion, a willingness to allow to others the liberty of thought we want for ourselves.

Patience. Sustained endurance of what is unpleasant, without petulance.

Organization. Unity of service among a number of persons in order to attain a common desired end.

Patriotism. Such devotion to one's country as tends to make it of greatest benefit to the citizens of it and to humanity in general.

Death. The cessation of the sensible phenomena of life.

Soul. The word applied to the personality of a human being implying that it is in reality spiritual and not material.

Conviction. The automatic conclusion of the mind after honest consideration of evidence.

Belief. A word sometimes used for the result of weighing evidence, and sometimes for a fancy that we adopt to gratify our emotions.

Prejudice. An opinion formed without considering evidence; usually to gratify our emotions.

Superstition. A morbid obsession, based upon no evidence.

Decision. A formation of opinion, or an act of the will, usually made by an intelligent weighing of probabilities.

Certainty. A state of mind possible only in regard to the mechanical, material, and lower elements of life. Affairs of deeper importance must be decided by probabilities.

Life. The open secret, the common mystery, the most important and the least understood of the forces of the universe.

THE FANATIC AND THE IDEALIST

Volume 2

What is the difference between the idealist and the fanatic? Simply this, that in the fanatic is a "missing link." He fails to connect his knowledge of what ought to be with his knowledge of what is.

The most beautiful of fanatics is probably the anarchist. I do not mean the depraved creatures who have no idea of what anarchy really is, and only borrow the word to cover their irresponsible vicious instincts; they have no more right to the name of anarchist than a bloody inquisitor of the year 1200, pouring molten lead into a heretic's ear, had a right to call himself a Christian.

I mean the apostles of the vision that the ideal condition of the race is that of having no outward law, each man being a law unto himself.

This will undoubtedly be mankind's millennial condition. It is in line with the scriptural prophecy that the days shall come when the laws shall no more be written upon tablets, but the Lord shall write them upon our hearts.

Now, as long as one has this vision, believes it, and works toward it, yet recognizes the facts and imperfections of humanity as it really is today, and seeks to connect his dream with actual conditions, he is an idealist, and does us all good.

But when he is so drunk with his vision that he tells us to smash all existing society, and that we are utterly rotten and hopeless, he is a fanatic. He forgets that whatever the future of the race is to be it must grow out of the present.

FEAR OF GREATNESS

Volume 4

Don't be afraid of your generous emotions.

The worst fear is the fear to be too great.

The meanest satisfaction is to be content in being like others.

If you trust a friend, trust him unto death. Of course you may be deceived in him. But better be humiliated by betrayal than be incapable of perfect faith.

If you love your wife, love loyally, utterly. She may not appreciate it. But better be unappreciated than to miss the joy of perfect self-giving.

Don't be too afraid of casting your pearls before swine. Better that than to hoard your pearls. And Jesus, who said it, did cast His pearls before many swine.

Don't be afraid to forgive. The object of your forgiveness may be unworthy, but that cannot mar the fineness of your pardon.

Don't be afraid to show yourself friendly, for only so you show yourself worth friendship.

Don't be afraid to believe in goodness. Better that evil should come as a shock than that you should have trusted in it.

Don't be afraid of being too kind. "In this world," says Marivaux, "one must be a little too kind to be kind enough."

THE FOOL

Volume 8

A fool is one who has no feeling of the future.

He is not a criminal; he is a child. It is not evil that ails him; it is arrested development.

The child wants everything now.

Tomorrow is vague to him, and has no appeal. He wants to stuff himself with green apples, and refuses to consider the consequent gripes.

And the gentleman in the dress-shirt who says he "wants what he wants when he wants it" is nothing but a child. When a child grows up, and doesn't grow up, he is called a fool.

The best part of anyone's life is the future. It is that which determines the quality of the present, and gives significance to the past. Tomorrow is the sky of today, and it is the sky that gives light and beauty and warmth to the earth.

Happy people live in the future, really happy people. Hope is a much more dominant factor in the joy of life than gratification. In the old question they used to debate in the high school: "Resolved, that there is more pleasure in anticipation than in possession." The affirmative has it.

The fool slaughters the goose to get the golden egg. Hence continual boredom.

Pessimism is kept active by fools. For the man who never takes care for the future naturally does not look forward to it.

The secret of the wise-hearted is: "Look out for tomorrow, and today will look out for itself."

The standard fool was Esau, who sold his birthright for a mess of pottage.

The streets of the city are full of his descendants, girls buying months and years of wretchedness for an hour of smiles and preening, boys buying floods of shame and failure for a few bottles of passion.

"Eat, drink, and be merry, for tomorrow we die"—you flatter yourself; tomorrow you will live, which is worse than death.

Tomorrow is the best counselor, the truest friend.

Whoever walks and talks with him will get the most out of today.

"I will lift mine eyes unto the hills, from whence cometh my strength," said a sage. The name of that range of hills is tomorrow.

The fool's creed is:

"I believe in Now. I believe appetites were made to be gratified and not to be controlled. I believe in having a good time, for I'll never be young but once. I believe in mortgaging every acre of the future and using the money now. I believe in picking all the blossoms and never caring for the fruit. I believe in looking out for number one. I believe in other people being thrifty, self-restrained, and temperate, for my benefit. I believe in luck. I believe no one ever really got on by hard work, but that success is a throw of the dice. I believe the rich are happy. I believe I do not need advice. I believe in always being kind, thoughtful, liberal, and charitable—to myself."

FORGET IT

It's over now. It's done. Forget it! Don't forever be raking it up, thinking it over, wishing you had done differently.

Forget it!

What's done's done. It's down in the bottomless pit of the past. Let it be!

Look ahead, not behind!

Think of tomorrow, not yesterday!

You can make something of tomorrow; yesterday is beyond recall.

Yesterday's as dead as a doornail, as lifeless as a brick, as hopeless and unchangeable as wood. Turn away from it!

Tomorrow's alive, pregnant with beauty, radiant with power, bulging with all conceivable possibilities. Turn to it!

"Forgetting those things which are behind, and reaching forth unto those things which are before," is the way one of the greatest souls of earth described his attitude.

For the past is dead. The future is life.

From the past come up the miasms of despair, remorse, self-contempt, which sickly o'er the thought, until the zone of purpose is loosed, and the high star is quenched in murky cloud.

Forget it, woman! You've sinned. Out of your weakness you have plucked loathing, and out of your waywardness shame. But it's done. Look not back at it. Look forward, to where One stands, One who, though He be judge of all the earth, says: "Go, and sin no more!"

Forget it, boy. You've brought tears to the eyes of her that bore you, and anguished care to your mother, than whom none in heaven or earth has greater love. But she will think of it no more if you only come back, put your face upon her blessed knees, and let her love enfold you. Hers is oblivion's widest, deepest sea, and your every offense will be drowned in it.

Forget it, man! Take her back into your arms. What is love worth that cannot forgive? What is love worth that is not mightier than pride? Forget it! In the streets of heaven you will never blush to think you have forgiven too much.

Forget it, wife! I know it means heartache and humiliation and dry-lipped care; but climb up, climb up the steeps of grandeur, till you reach the stage of that love which "beareth all things, believeth all things, hopeth all things, endureth all things—and never faileth."

Once in the mountain air of nobleness you will not regret the troubled valleys of pride.

Forget it! Everybody! Every

uprolling sun brings a new chance to all the sons and daughters of men. Every swelling moon means a new month of opportunity. Every star of the innumerable stars, sand-strewn on the dusky blue of night, is a star of hope.

Forget it! Front face, you!

FROM THE CHIN UP

Volume 7

From your chin down you are worth about a dollar and a half a day.

From the chin up you are worth—anything. There's no limit.

Without your headpiece you are just an animal, and about as valuable as a horse—maybe.

You have a mistaken idea. You think you are paid for your work. You are not. You are paid for what you think while you work. It's the kind of brain that directs your hands that gives you your rating.

And what causes you the most concern: the contents of your skull, or the mass below the collar-bone?

You exercise your body, keep your arms strong, and your legs limber, and your waistline supple—but do you regularly exercise your cerebrum? Are your thoughts flabby, uncon-trolled, wayward, and useless, though you are expert in tennis or golf?

Is your thinker as keen, alert, disciplined, accurate, and depend-able as your hands?

Where do you get your plea-sures? From the chin down? Is it all dancing for your feet, and meat for your belly, and clothes for your back? And—is all your fun in the cellar? Don't you ever have any fun in the attic?

What interests you most, books or beer?

What pains your most, a stom-achache or a lie?

How are you pulled? To what part of you is the cable-tow fas-tened—to your loins or to your forehead?

Suppose it were possible to live after the head had been severed from the body; which part would you rather be, the head part or the meat part?

What are you, anyhow: an ani-mal, pestered with a mind; or a soul, prisoned in a body?

Do you know that the gist of culture consists in transferring one's habitual amusements from below to above the nose?

A good definition of a fool is one who thinks this time doesn't count.

—THE COMEBACK

THE GENTLEMAN

Volume 1

What makes a gentleman? Not clothes, of course. And not any outward thing, even manners and smooth words. A monkey might also be trained to sip soup from the side of the spoon, not to eat with his knife, and to enter a room properly. And a man may have breeding and culture and wisdom and still miss being a gentleman. What, then, constitutes a gentleman?

There are two essential elements. First, there must be a man; and second, he must be gentle.

First, then, he must be brave, not with physical lack of nerves, but unafraid in his heart, seeing the laws of truth and goodness and committing himself to them with utter indifference to consequences.

Second, he must be gentle; that is, he must have learned to use his courage kindly.

Bravery is the masculine characteristic; gentleness the feminine. The man comes first, we say; the woman after. True enough, but the woman is the finishing, perfecting element. What we call civilization is nothing but the womanization of a race. Those races are extinguished in the process who do not have sufficient masculinity to stand it.

When you have a brave man who is not gentle, you have a barbarian; noble, possibly, great and strong, but still a savage. When you have a gentle soul that is not brave, that dare not risk the higher verities, you have no man at all, but a milksop. But when you have a man who is profoundly fearless, and who has also learned to be gentle, then you have that finest product of God's handiwork of which we have any definite knowledge—a gentleman.

GO ON

Volume 5

There are some men who can obey orders; and there are some men who can get things done.

It is well to be obedient; it is better to be resourceful.

When Alexander could not untie the Gordian knot he cut it with his sword.

A resourceful man is one who, when he cannot do a thing one way, does it another.

He keeps trying.

When it's time to quit, he begins.

When he is licked, he begins fighting again.

Success in life is not like shooting at a mark with a rifle; it is like trying to hit a mark with a stream of water from a hose; you just keep on till finally you hit it—maybe.

It is well to know how; it is better to try; for by trying you learn how.

Success is like picking a lock, not like working an example in long division.

It is like solving a rebus more than it is like demonstrating a theorem in geometry.

It is like starting a fire with damp wood more than it is like getting a chemical reaction in a laboratory.

It is like fitting together the pieces of a torn letter more than it is like building a wall of bricks.

All the big things are accomplished by trying, trying, trying. Only the little things can be done by rule, and a cheap hand to do them.

To paint a great picture means infinite approximations. None is painted by rule.

Nobody learns to write well, except by writing. Only by keeping everlastingly at it, whether we feel like it or not, with inspiration and without, in quiet and in din, in comfort and in dyspepsia, "no day without a line," only so comes the mysterious endowment of style.

The man who fails is not the man who has no gift, no chance, no pull, no encouragement, no training; it is the man who quits.

Genius is the inexhaustible capacity for going on.

Training, education, and the like before you go to work is valuable; but it is the training and education you get by and while doing your work that counts most.

There are three rules for success. The first is: Go on. The second is: Go on. And the third is: Go on.

You can't win a woman by the rules of a book, nor can you make biscuit, nor get elected to office, nor build up a trade, nor get yourself liked, nor achieve contentment, nor get to heaven.

Life is an endless experiment.

Wisdom is the precipitate of experiment.

Belief is the spirit of experiment.

Character is the subjective result of experiment.

And success the objective result. Go on!

Liberty is a boat we're all in. A leak anywhere will sink it.

—THE PRICE OF LIBERTY

GOD'S WHISPER

A nybody might have heard it, but God's whisper came to me," says the poet.

God always whispers. At least to the soul. He may thunder to nations and speak to armies in the lightning. But to the individual His message is not in the mighty wind, nor the earthquake, nor the fire, but in the still, small voice.

God lives in the bottom of the funnel of silence.

He is the treasure concealed in solitude.

He meets men alone, in the dark.

Congregations have their use, and books, and papers, and multitudes, and friends, but God loves the silent way.

He is every soul's most secret secret.

If, as Thoreau said, it takes two to tell the truth, it takes also two to make a revelation; it takes the whisper of God and the listening man.

God's whisper runs to and fro upon the earth. It might be heard in all cottages, palaces, marts, offices, inns, and councils—if only we listened.

Go into the silence. Give your soul time to calm. Let the hurly-burly die down, the crash of passion, the struggle of doubt, the pain of failure, the ranklings of wrong, the clamor of ambition. Cease from self. Be still.

Practise this. It is an art, and not to be mastered out of hand. Try it again and again, as patiently, as determinedly, as lovingly as one practises the violin or the making of a statue.

And after a while, as virtuosity comes after long trials, there will come to life in you the needed sixth sense, by which you can hear the whisper.

Some day you will get it. It may rise like a strange dawn in your consciousness. It may stir in you as life stirs in the egg. It may penetrate the deep chambers of your being as a strain of mystic music.

And it will be the prize of life. You will not be able to give it to another. Every man must receive such things himself. All of God's most vital secrets are marked non-transferable.

But it will be yours—that which in all your life is most utterly yours.

It will strengthen you in weakness, cheer you in hours of gloom. When you are at sea and confused, lost in the winds of casuistry, it will shine out as a pole-star. When you are afraid, it will reinforce you as an army with banners.

It will lull you to sleep with its music. It will give you poise. It will give you decision.

No man can tell what the whisper says. Each soul must hear for itself.

That is a great secret. One can only point the way—the way is silence.

There stands God and says: "I will give to eat of the hidden manna, and will give him a white stone, and in the stone a new name written, which no man knoweth saving he that receiveth it. He that hath an ear, let him hear what the Spirit saith."

GREAT LOVE AND MUCH SERVICE

It is the commonest things in the world that most need definition.

There are certain vital subjects the mind handles every day, indeed must handle because they are as essential to thought as bread and water to the body; and by much handling these subjects become smooth as old coins. Once in a while it is well to examine them minutely to see what "image and superscription" is thereon.

Nothing is more constantly spoken of than happiness. It is the end of religion, the object of philosophy, the dream of the wretched, the quest of the whole world.

BUT WHAT IS IT?

Suppose we ask ourselves that? And suppose we patiently and honestly try to find an answer? If we discover what happiness is, or at least what it means to us, we have gone a long way toward grasping happiness, the thing itself.

And just to stimulate your inquiry allow me to hand to you a definition I read the other day, I know not where. It is this:

"Happiness is great love and much service."

If you will look about carefully among the people you know, not neglecting yourself, you will discover that not one of them is happy that does not love. Furthermore that all of them are happy in proportion as they love.

Happiness is the perfume of the rose of love, the light shining from the candle of love, the sound from the bells of love.

You can get a certain something that resembles happiness from the gratification of desire, from eating, drinking, playing, and the like. But it all has in itself the seed of boredom. You get SATED from satisfying appetite; but in the happiness that comes from love is no satiety.

What is true of love is equally true of service; because to love is to serve.

Search again among the people

you know, and note that they are happy in proportion as they serve.

The great mass of men and women are reasonably content because they are at work.

They often complain of their work. They even call labor a curse. But they would be miserable without it.

They dream of a life of idleness and self-indulgence, and many imagine that is heaven. It is not. It is hell.

This world was made for lovers and for servants.

If any one's heart is full of love, and his hand is full of service, he has no morbid "problems." He has solved the riddle of life.

THE GREAT MAN

Volume 1

The great man feels with the people, but does not follow them.

He maintains his independence of thought, no matter what public opinion may be.

His is quiet. He does not strive nor cry out.

He knows and trusts the cosmic spiritual forces and is not impatient.

He thinks clearly, he speaks intelligently, he lives simply.

His ethics are of the future, not traditional and of the past, nor conventional and of the present.

He always has time.

He despises no human being, nor any other creature.

He impresses you much as the vast silences of nature impress you; as the sky, the ocean, the desert.

He has no vanity. Seeking no praise, he is never offended. He always has more than he thinks he deserves.

He is teachable, and will learn even from little children. He is not anxious to teach others.

He is not welcome in any sect, cult or party, for he is more desirous of understanding than of opposing the other party.

He is rarely elected to anything.

He works for the joy of it, not the wages.

He cannot retaliate, for he cannot descend to the level of them that love to do harm.

He lives in a certain self-sufficient aloofness, so that your praise or blame does not seem to reach him.

Yet his isolation is warm, and not cold.

He is keenly alive to human relationships and influences. He loves. He cares. He suffers. He laughs.

When you find him it is as if

you had found a real human being among myriads of animals. All of the simple, strong qualities of the normal soul shine in him, with no pettiness.

You feel that what you have, such as your money or position, is nothing to him, only what you are; and that if he likes you it will be not at all for anything you do, say, or pay, but for what your soul is within you.

He is not deceived by the two arrant humbugs of the world, success and failure.

He changes his opinion easily, when he sees his error. He cares not for consistency, which is the fetich of little minds, but for truth, which is the sum of great souls.

He believes that every man comes at last unto his own, and is not impatient.

Bitterness, cynicism, and pessimism, which are tempers of pettiness, he has not; but love, cheer, and hope abound in him, for these are always the by-products of greatness.

When you love him, you yourself become great; for there can be no greatness that is not the cause of greatness in others.

THE GREAT SILENCES

Volume 1

Have you ever thought of the great silences? They are the sources of our deepest, our sublimest feeling. From them all superior souls draw their habitual sustenance.

There is the silence of the sky. Who has not felt a sense of awe pervade him, a breath of fearsome grandeur breathe through him, as he has looked up at the stars—remote, silent worlds that know us not?

There is the silence of the night, when the last bird is asleep, and even the wind has ceased to whisper, and the whole world stands black and "breathless as a nun." What thoughts come then, looming portentously!

There is the silence of the sea, a huge white continent of water flashing in the sun, containing what noiseless deeps and monsters!

There is the silence of art, the mute appeal of the Venus de Milo, of [the] Mona Lisa, of the Sistine Madonna.

There is the silence of grief, more terrible than its noisy tears, more appalling than shrieks of agony, that terrible stillness of heartbreak.

There is the silence of the dead, most difficult of all to grasp. How can those lips be forever still?

There is the silence of God. The mightiest of all forces, the most marvellous of all personalities is stillest of all. His is the "still, small voice."

And best and greatest of all is the silence of love, which is "the sun of love, and ripens the fruit of the soul."

"Bees," says Carlyle, "will not work except in darkness; thought will not work except in silence; nor virtue except in secrecy."

THE GREAT SOUL

Volume 7

Not everyone will profess that he wants to be good, but all admit they would like to be great.

And greatness, although a secret matter, is yet well known; it has had its masters, examples, and teachers, and whosoever will may attain unto it.

Herein lie the secrets of being great.

The great soul has its resources within itself; the small soul looks to outside things and other people.

The great soul asks, "What is true?" The small soul, "What is expedient?"

The great soul is radical, he seeks for causes; the small soul is superficial, he sees only symptoms.

The great soul is of hospitable mind; the small soul clings to prejudices.

The great soul cares only that he be sincere; the small soul that he produce a desired effect.

The great soul is honest with himself; the small soul is satisfied with honesty toward others.

The great soul can concentrate; the small is dissipated.

The great soul dominates his environment; the small soul is dominated by it.

The great soul has decision; the small soul constantly hesitates.

The great soul has poise; the small soul is ever unbalanced.

The great soul has principles; the small soul policies.

The great soul learns the general laws that run through the universe, and trusts them even against appearances; the small soul sees only the present profit and loss and hence is confused and can neither believe nor understand.

The great soul is above worry; the small soul is burdened by it.

The great soul has no fear; the small soul is harassed by fears continually.

The great soul lives easily—that

is, with dignity and calmness of mind; the small soul is readily upset.

The great soul speaks concisely and his yea is yea; the small wrangles.

The great soul first makes sure he is right and is then firm; the small soul is first firm and then casts about for reasons for being so.

The great soul is sincerely humble; the small soul is vain.

The great soul is appreciative of all; the small soul is flattering toward those from whom he seeks some favor, negligent or insolent toward those who cannot contribute to his advancement.

The great soul is temperate in all things; the small soul intemperate in his beliefs, his opinions, and his tastes.

The great soul has the atmosphere of charity, is tolerant toward all, and helpful in the very character of his life; the small soul is satisfied with acts of charity.

What impresses you in the great soul is his reserve power; in the small soul the performance or the word seems greater than the man.

Says the Chinese Li Ki, "The services of Hau Ki were the most meritorious of all under heaven. But all he longed for was that his actions should be better than the fame of them."

The Greatest Enemy

Fear is the greatest enemy to the human soul.

At the bottom of almost every inflammation of the ego is a little pus-point of fear. If one can but prick that he is on the way to cure.

Every sin, every sorrow, every crime and shadow that lies upon man or woman may be expressed in terms of fear.

What indescribable misery has been caused by the fear of God! From that came the long dark centuries when the world lay tormented by the nightmare of superstition and intolerance. Fear is the father of cruelty. Fear dehumanizes. When the devil can make us afraid we are right to his hand. It is when they are in a panic of fear that the rattlesnake strikes, the dog bites, the horse runs away, the cat scratches, the bee stings, the scorpion attacks, the bull gores, the woman lies, the man kills.

Fear is the devil's other name.

In a mob-panic men become fiends. It is fear that makes the

ship-captain brutal, the slave-driver inhuman, the warden's punishments hard and hideous.

Fear has led mothers to burn their children in idolatrous fires, priests to practise human sacrifice.

All the schrecklichkeit* of the mad war in Europe is but the obverse side of fear. It is not courage that torpedoes the *Lusitania,* destroys innocent non-combatants with Zepelin bombs, uses asphyxiating gas, outrages women, maims little children, refuses food to the starving population of a conquered territory, and sets typhoid germs in prison camps; it is frantic fear. Turn fear over, and its other side, you will see, is cruelty.

It is from fear—fear of the sneers of his fellows— that the youth poisons himself with alcohol, loses his money gambling, and taints his body in the house of death.

Worry is a form of fear, fear of the future, of the purpose of destiny, of the grudge of God, of the sinister design of fate.

Fear of poverty—how it has unloosed the zone of women, and made cads and crooks of honorable men!

Awkwardness—what is it but fear of others, making us unlovely, boorish? What an ugly garment is the investment of fear!

Fear is probably the cause of stammering, of all unpleasant mannerisms.

Shyness and sensitiveness cause us a deal of misery and rob us of much contentment and ease that by right should be ours. They are but fear forms.

Jealousy, chief of heart-breakers and love-wreckers, is the fear of love, the fierce opposite of courageous trust.

And finally monarchy, tyranny, absolutism are but fear of the people. It takes a very high courage to maintain a democracy.

No better word can be inscribed on the shield of youth, going forth to find happiness and the golden dream, than that which Jehovah gave to Joshua when he led his people into the promised land:

"Only be thou strong and of a good courage; be not afraid, neither be thou dismayed; for the Eternal is with thee whithersoever thou goest."

When I say that another made me do an evil thing I lie to myself. Others may have threatened, cajoled, tempted, pushed, or bribed me, but the fatal final step was never taken except by the consent of my own will.

—LYING TO YOURSELF

*terror

GREATNESS

The greatness of a man lies in his ability to interpret his age.

Such a man must have that rarest of traits of genius; he must instinctively feel his fellow-men.

He is not a leader. The whole strongman theory is a humbug. He is a servant.

The greatest man is the man who comes nearest to executing the will of the people. He is "servant of all."

If he is a poet, he utters the word they dumbly feel. If he is an artist, he bodies forth their impotent fancy. If he is a statesman, he materializes their political convictions. If he is an orator or a writer, he says what they all would say. Always behind him is the mass, from which he draws his force.

It is this power of submerging one's self in the current of others' feeling that is the gift of greatness.

The lawyer is great who loses himself in the interests of his clients.

The physician is great who gives himself up to his patients, serving the poorest of them as loyally as any subject ever served his king.

The teacher is great who is the exponent of his pupils, the expression of their intellectual curiosity, the will of their highest ambitions.

The workman is great who feels the profit of his employer, the care of his goods, and the perfecting of his work as if it were his own.

The merchant is great who senses his customers, divines their needs, ministers to their wants; and he is greater yet if he feels his responsibility to those he employs, if he is the personal embodiment of the activities of all his working force.

A president, a governor, a senator, a congressman, a mayor, is great if he knows his people; if their conscience is his conscience; if his voice is their thought; if their desires and ideals move his hand and brain.

Homer, Goethe, Voltaire, Shakespeare, spoke their time.

The great men are the manufacture of the people.

David, Cæsar, Washington, Napoleon—these knew how to ride the crest of the multitudinous wave.

Even of Jesus no greater thing can be said than that He uttered the heart of all mankind.

A wise man will not seek peace without, but peace within.
—PEACE WITHIN

THE HABIT OF SELF-CONFIDENCE

—————————————————————————————*Volume 6*

Like almost everything else, self-confidence is a habit.

It is formed by persistently choosing to let the mind dwell upon our successes, and in turning our thoughts just as persistently away from our failures.

Suppose out of the ten things you did today eight were failures. When you come at the end of the day's doings to take stock give these eight one good look, don't dodge them, see what caused them and how you may do better tomorrow—and then dismiss them from your mind.

Think of the two things wherein you have succeeded, even if they be of small import. Speak of them. Don't mention the others.

Keep bringing your success episodes up into the light and air, where they can grown and reproduce their kind. And keep the failure incidents as much as possible in the cellar of your memory, in the dark, where they will "dwindle, peak, and pine." Sterilize your failures. Asphyxiate them.

Of course, this is easier said than done. What hurts is more easily and sharply remembered than what pleases.

A slap in the face is harder to forget than a pat on the back.

Bad things, unpleasant things, ugly things, and nasty things have a way of sticking to us; and good, pleasant, beautiful, and wholesome things, such as our conceit,* we are prone to take as matters of course and pay little attention to them.

But here precisely is where the will comes in. Here is the opportunity for self-training. Here is the secret of improvableness.

For moral slumping is always easy and moral bracing hard. "Smooth is the road to hell," runs the proverb. A person with a flabby will is growing worse every day, just as a man that will not pull at the oars is steadily floating downstream.

And a man is never more a man than when he summons up his will to combat a tendency.

As a matter of fact, almost every day for every one of us contains more agreeable than disagreeable things, even to the grouchiest of souls. Just take a pencil and paper and set down in one column all the events of the day, big and little, that have gratified you, and in another all that have annoyed you; and if you are honest in your account you will find the first column has ten items to the other's one.

The trouble is that the one offensive occurrence magnifies itself. The one point on your body where

*thought

you have a boil attracts more of your attention than the entire remaining surface.

And when a child has a sore he wants to pick it. And we love to handle over and over the memory of the thing that hurt or pained us.

Well, quit!

Turn around!

Back up!

Except you be converted (which is a Latinish word that means turned around) ye cannot see the Kingdom.

Let the inflamed spots in your recollection alone. When the rebuff, or mistake, or loss, or insult, or slight, or other ugly thing soever pops up in your thinking, look away, direct your thoughts elsewhere.

It is hard to do. But all improvement is hard.

The only way to climb any height of culture is to keep on doing a difficult thing until it becomes easy.

And the very heart and core secret of culture is to have the disposition to tackle the difficult things.

Half-Science

There is a kind of bastard science which is very dangerous.

It gets a glimpse of the great law of "The Survival of the Fittest." It explains so many things. And the apprentice mind in its enthusiasm imagines it explains everything.

It does not. The Survival of the Fittest, the Struggle for Existence, and the whole law that the physically weak are exterminated and the physically strong survive, all this is true only up to a certain point.

It is true of tigers and tomcats; it is not true of human beings.

When man appeared, in the history of evolution, he brought another element into the arena, the moral element.

Not to reckon with this moral power is not to be a scientist, but a half-scientist.

The German mind is half-scientific. That is what ails it. It conceives that the final triumph will rest with "the big blond beast," with the men of muscle and ferocity, with those who thrust aside all motives of pity and gentleness and concentrate on material force.

The saying that "God is on the side of the strongest battalions," is a sample of this half-reasoning.

God is on the side of truth, honor, humaneness, and love; and in the end these gentle powers shall overcome. That is what Jesus meant when He said that "the meek shall inherit the earth." And that is what the half-baked mind sneers at, neither indeed can believe.

But just the same, Civilization means the superiority of the moral forces and the eventual subjugation of all Brute force.

The present war is a struggle between the moral and the brute ideas.

Civilization is not a working out of materialistic laws; it is the mastery and direction of those laws by a spiritual, non-material something called Man.

HEAVEN HELP THE POOR

Volume 2

Heaven help the poor! I do not mean the poor in money. For the greatest of earth have thus been poor—Socrates, Wagner, Rousseau, Poe, Lincoln, Whitman, and Jesus poorest of all, who had not where to lay His head.

I mean poor in resources.

For the only poverty that grinds, deadens, and kills is poverty of resources.

When sorrow comes the poor in resources have no wells of inner happiness from which to draw.

When their money is gone they have no inner riches.

When they drop from their station in life they know no human beings to turn to.

When they are bereaved they have no tides of faith to support them.

They are poor in self-mastery, and their environment overcomes them.

They are poor in discipline, and their own selves fall upon them and devour them.

They are poor in enthusiasms, and when their one little interest is gone they have no other.

They are poor in friends, and to their calamity is added loneliness.

They are poor in passion, and to a love-hungry world they have nothing to offer.

They are poor in thoughts, and, as Robert Louis Stevenson says, do not have so much as two ideas to rub against each other while waiting for a train.

They are poor in work, having never found their task, without which no soul can be happy.

They are poor in time, having smothered creative leisure by the clutter of the unimportant.

They are poor in beauty, having never learned to see it, let alone feed upon it.

These are the wretched ones of the earth. They stand, shivering souls looking in through the window at the warmth of life; hungry souls begging of every passerby the bread of praise which they cannot digest.

It's hell to be poor, poor in all that makes life rich and strong and easy.

It's pitiful, too, to see poverty-stricken souls trying to buy real riches with money, whereat the gods laugh.

"Wherefore do ye spend money for that which is not bread? and your labour for that which satisfieth not? hearken diligently unto me, and eat ye that which is good, and let your soul delight itself in fatness."

HEROISM

Heroism is the salt that keeps humanity from rotting.

When we take an inventory of the qualities and passions of the crowd we are likely to find a discouraging state of things. They who despise the human race are not without their reasons.

What a welter of selfishness in the business world, what treacheries and cruelties, often what utter heartlessness and brute seizures!

In the relations between men and women what a world of sickening facts!

In family life what jars and pettiness, what frequent degradation of what should be the most beautiful and most ideal of human relationships!

In the history of religion what a shameful list of perversions; headstrongness, vanity, intolerance, persecution, superstition, and even wolfish passions!

But all these are salted and cured, altered and antidoted, by one thing—heroism.

Not the spectacular kind that makes the commons gape; but the unknown, unseen kind, done for itself alone, for the eye of God and the satisfaction of a noble self-respect.

Think of the unnoted and unnumbered acts of heroism on the part of mothers! These alone would save the world, as ten good men would have saved Sodom.

Look (and if you seek you shall find) at the numberless deeds of self-sacrifice among the poor, the self-renunciations of the rich, the helpfulness of fellow-workmen, the splendid courage of men and women that they often conceal with a sense of shame!

True, friend pessimist, humanity may be just mud, dirt, earth; but all through it sparkles the pure and priceless gold of heroism.

HIDDEN HAPPINESS

Volume 7

Happiness is rarely visible to the multitude, says a shrewd observer; it lies hidden in odd corners and quiet places.

Happiness is a shy thing. Grief is blatant and advertising. If a boy cuts his finger he howls, proclaiming his woe. If he is eating pie he sits still and says nothing.

If you ask a man how he is, he searches himself to find a pain to report. If he has nothing but happiness he hates to mention it, and says, "Oh, not half bad."

We conceal happiness, as a vice.

We are rather suspicious of it, and if we feel particularly well, or have exceptional good luck, we knock on wood.

The fact is that happiness does not come from the big events of life, but is made up of innumerable little things.

Ordinary every-day happiness is composed of shoes that fit, stomach that digests, purse that does not flatten, a little appreciation, and a bit of this, that, and the other, too trifling to mention.

The big things, such as someone giving you a million dollars, are not only rare, but they do not satisfy when you have the neuritis.

We are so cantankerous by nature that we are usually able to spell happiness only by holding it before the mirror and reading backwards. Leonardo da Vinci used to write that way; that may be why he could paint "The Joyous One" with so enigmatical a smile.

For if you seek to analyze contentment you go at it negatively. To feel well means you do not have headache, toothache, nor toeache, you have no dyspepsia, catarrh, gout, sciatica, hives, nausea, boils, cancer, grippe, rhinitis, iritis, appendicitis, nor any other itis. And to determine your joy you must reckon by checking off and eliminating the factors of possible pain. Answer: happy, if no pain discoverable. So elusive is joy!

Someday try reversing this process. Note all the pleasurable things. For instance, a good sleep, a delightful snooze in bed after you ought to get up, a delicious bath, the invigorating caress of cold water, a good breakfast, with somebody you love visible across the coffee-cups, a half-hour's diversion with the newspaper, the flash of nature's loveliness outdoors as you go to work, interesting faces on the street car, pleasures of your business, pleasant relations with your fellow-workers, meeting old friends and new faces, the good story someone tells you, and so on—you'll fill your notebook—and you can get your disappointments and grievances into three lines.

Happiness, they say, is scant in this wicked world and hard to find.

One way to find it is to look for it.

How to Keep Friends

Volume 3

It is a deal easier to make friends than to keep them.

A pretty way, a clever mind, a jovial mood, a generous impulse, a happy occasion can be cause enough to arouse your interest in a person at first encounter, and you go away saying: "I like that fellow," or "I like that girl."

The real friend grows upon you.

At first you may be indifferent. He may even repel you. He may be gruff, or reserved, or have some odd corners that jag you. Perhaps he's so quiet he seems stupid. Belike he has radical views which he announces belligerently. Or he may appear cynical, or too prim, or loquacious, or supercilious, or egotistic.

But time tells. You are thrown with him again and again. You may have to work with him, or play with him, or meet him at the club or table or group. And by and by you realize that you fit, you two.

You can get along with each other, meaning that you do not rasp. He does not irritate you. You do not have to be always "holding yourself in" when he is around.

Not that you admire him necessarily. Some of our most congenial friends are those of whom we heartily disapprove. You may be fully alive to his limitations, but somehow they do not annoy you.

And having acquired a friend it is important not to lose him. One way of getting rid of a friend is to expect too much of him.

You may feel he would do anything for you. But be careful; don't ask him for favors. Just content yourself with the pleasing belief that he would do anything for you.

Don't set traps for him. Don't

say, "I will ask him to do so and so, and test his friendship." Whosoever tempts a friend is unworthy of friendship.

Don't ask him to go out of his way to accommodate you. Don't presume upon his good nature.

"No one," says Ed Howe, "has ever done much for me. I may have expected a great deal from friends long ago, but I do not now. I have not only learned that if I expect a great deal of them I will be disappointed; I have learned that I have no right to expect it. Friends are like a pleasant park where you wish to go; while you may enjoy the flowers, you must not cut them."

You will be much more likely to keep friends if you never try to sell them anything, never have money dealings with them, never advise them in any matter where they may possibly lose money, and in short eliminate the dollar entirely from your dealings with them.

Another pretty sure method of losing friends is to strive to improve them. Do all your uplift work with your enemies. Take for friends those who suit you just as they are.

HOW TO LIVE A HUNDRED YEARS

Volume 3

Of course there is no recipe for living a hundred years. What we mean, in sober and careful language, is how to keep the body machine in such good condition that, barring accidents, we shall round out our appointed term of life in health and vigor.

To accomplish this there is nothing new to suggest, either in nostrum or health program; but we need to be reminded of those established rules that are the result of universal experience, and of the application of intelligence to life. Hence, observe the following:

Eat intelligently. Learn the nutritive values of foods. Eat what you need. Let the diet be simple. Avoid satiety; quit eating before you are sated. Chew well.

Drink only pure water. Water containing certain salts and minerals may be beneficial; ask your physician. Drink a plenty. Water is man's greatest friend in nature.

Keep clean. Bathe regularly.

Sweat often. If you cannot afford Turkish baths get a bath-cabinet of your own, or make one, and perspire freely at least once a week. Thorough perspiration is the salvation of the kidneys.

Take regularly no alcohol in

any form. There is no use in open-ing this subject again. The regular drinker of alcoholic beverages is a foolish person. He is purchasing a pleasant glow at the expense of in-viting a hundred disorders.

Be out of doors as much as you can. Fresh air, sunshine, and water are nature's three cure-alls. Sleep with your windows open summer and winter.

Exercise systematically. Modern life is as a rule so routined that the muscles and organs of the body are not harmoniously developed. There are many books and teachers of ex-ercise; but the principles are few, and usually the same in all systems. It is regular, not occasional and vio-lent, exercise that counts.

Avoid constipation, one of the most prolific sources of bodily de-rangement. Take the matter up se-riously with your physician.

Avoid excesses of any kind. Be temperate in all things.

Maintaining the body in a state of efficiency is largely a matter of thought training. This truth is be-ing emphasized a great deal nowa-days, and rightly so.

Don't worry. It is mostly a mat-ter of habit. Don't get into the way of it. Worry is the prime life-short-ener.

Don't indulge in hate. Don't al-low yourself to entertain a grudge against any human being. What's the use? Forget it.

Don't give way to regrets for the past, nor to premonitions of evil for the future.

Keep the mind cheerful. Play and laugh as much as you can.

Have some part of the world's work to do. Feel that you are earn-ing your salt. Be interested in some constructive and useful activity.

Work at your life by the day and not by the job. Be satisfied with each day's results.

Marry; have children; the most wholesome class of people in the world are grandfathers and grand-mothers.

Believe in the almightiness of goodness and shun any success that involves a troubled conscience.

These probably sound like preachy platitudes to you; they are; but it is necessary to keep repeating them because we are constantly over-looking or discounting them; we need to be reminded that they are the best we yet know about the art of living a hundred years.

Humility is the only door by which wisdom and greatness and peace can enter, and it is usu-ally barred and bolted by pride and egotism.

—A SCHOOL FOR LIVING

HUMAN FLIES

Volume 10

Oh for a human fly-swatter! That is, for some sort of a swatter that would obliterate the human fly.

The most prominent trait of a fly is his ability and disposition to bother. He is essential, concentrated botheraciousness. He is the arch intruder. He is the type of the unwelcome. His business is to make you quit what you are doing and attend to him.

He makes the busy cook cease her breadmaking to shoo him away. He disturbs the sleeper to brush him off. He is president and chairman of the executive committee of the amalgamated association of all pesterers, irritators, and nuisances.

The human fly is the male or female of the genus homo who is like the housefly.

Some children are like flies. They are so ill bread and undisciplined that they perpetually annoy their mother until her nerves are frazzled, and make life miserable for any guests that may be in the house. It may be well to be kind and thoughtful toward the little darlings, but the first lesson a child should be taught is to govern himself as not to be a bother. There are respectful, considerate, and unobtrusive children—alas, too few!

There are fly wives. Realizing their own pettiness they gain their revenge by systematically irritating the husband. They make a weapon of their weakness. They soon acquire the art of pestering, nipping, and buzzing, keep the man in a perpetual temper, and blame him for it. You can't talk to them. Nothing can cure them but an eleven-foot swatter. And these are not for sale.

Some men are just as bad. Married to a superior woman such a man is inwardly galled by his own conscious inferiority. So he bedevils her in ways indirect. He enjoys seeing her in a state of suppressed indignation. He keeps her on edge. His persecution is all the more unbearable because it is the unconscious expression of his fly nature. Also for him there is no cure but to wait till he lights some time and swat him with some giant, gargantuan swatter. And they're all out of these, too, at the store.

There are office flies, likewise, who get into your room, occupy your extra chair, and buzz you for an hour upon some subject that you don't care a whoop in Halifax about. Your inherent politeness prevents you from kicking them out, humanity will not let you poison them, and there is a law against shooting them. There ought to be an open season for office flies.

Where the human flies are proudest in their function of pestiferousness, however, is in a meeting. Wherever you have a conference, a committee meeting, or a convention, there they buzz, tickle, and deblatterate. They keep the majority waiting while they air their incoherence. They suggest, amend, and raise objections. They never do anything; it is their business to annoy people who do things.

I do not wish to seem unkind to my fellow creatures, but it does seem as if to all legislatures, conventions, and other gatherings there should be an anteroom where the human flies could be gently but efficaciously swatted.

There are Senate flies, as well as House flies, politicians whose notion of their duty appears to be that they should vex, tantalize, and heckle the opposing party at every point.

There are fly newspapers, whose only policy seems to be petty, vicious annoyance. There are fly preachers, with a cheap efficiency in diatribe and sarcasm, and no wholesome, constructive message. There are fly school-teachers, who hector and scold; fly pupils, who find and fasten upon a teacher's sensitive spot; fly reformers, who can only make trouble; fly neighbors, who cannot mind their own business; fly shopkeepers, who will not let you buy what you want.

And the name of the devil himself is Beelzebub, which being interpreted means "Lord of Flies."

HUMANITY

Volume 2

What is my boasted independence? I am dependent upon everybody and everything. I go with the crowd. I am caught in the press of men. I must move with them.

All my ancestors have left me something. Not money or goods, but deeper potencies. What I call my character or nature is made up of infinite particles of inherited tendencies from those whose blood runs in my veins. A little seed of laziness from this grandfather and of prodigality from that. Some remote grandmother, perhaps, has stamped me with a fear of horses or a love of dogs. There may be in me a bit of outlawry from some forefather who was a pirate, and a dash of piety from one who was a saint.

So everything in me passes on through my children and flecks my children's children with a spot of strength or weakness. I am sewn in between ancestry and posterity. I am a drop of water in a flowing river. I am a molecule in a mountain. I am a cell in a great tree.

The words I think in are not mine. They are humanity's. Millions made them, as a coral reef into which my thoughts creep.

My gestures, ways, mannerisms, so-called peculiarities, I borrowed them all.

Religion is not a personal affair so much as it is a communal. You are a Jew because you were born a Jew; for the same reason you are a Catholic, you a Presbyterian, you a Mahometan, you a Buddist, you a Mormon. As we enter life we find these cells already made in the human beehive and crawl into them.

The young lover imagines no one else ever felt his pangs and ecstasies; yet Nature is but repeating in him the emotions she has made in a myriad others.

"Nothing human is alien to me," said the philosopher.

Said Burke, "Society is a partnership not only between those who are living, but between those who are living and those who are dead—and those who are to be born."

What I call my opinion—how much of it is but echo? Opinions are catching, like measles or smallpox. Our notions of art, letters, politics, morals, we have but secreted them from the mass.

Original ideas? Where will you find them? All the ideas there are exist now, floating in the human sea. I, an oyster, absorb a few, and call them mine. Even the phrases of the Lord's Prayer have been traced to Talmudic sources.

"The dewdrop slips into the shining sea." The river of humanity emerges from the infinite and pours ever into the infinite again.

In passing how we perk ourselves up into strange egotisms! We strut, gesticulate, contend, and talk of me and mine, only to go down at last in the cataract that, unceasing as Niagara, empties into the unknown.

Let us, therefore, put away the coarse egotisms and the partisan passions that infest us, and learn to love humanity, to think and feel in terms of humanity.

Happiness is not a thing at all, but is the relation between two things; that is, the relation between our condition and what we think our condition ought to be, between what we have and what we conceive to be our deserts.

—THE ROAD TO THANKFULNESS

I Don't Know

Volume 7

Certain plants never grow except in certain soils; edelweiss in the Alps, bananas in the tropics, and cacti in the sands of the desert. Wherever you find the plant called Humility in the human garden you will always discover real wisdom in the brain-soil that produces it.

The habit of positivity has the true flavor of ignorance, for if one is always certain he is usually wrong. Humbugs, impostors, frauds, and sciolists never hesitate; but when you talk to a man of genuine learning, mature experience, and thorough culture, such a man as Mark Hopkins or President Eliot, the thing that strikes you most in him is his almost childlike modesty.

When once you have learned that it is as sure a sign of wisdom to say you do not know as to say you do know, when you have learned that it is pretense and not ignorance that is shameful, when you want to be esteemed for nothing except what you really are, and to hate nothing so much as to be praised for what you are not, then you can be at ease in any company, everybody from servant to savant will enjoy you, and, as was said of Robert Burns, you will be equally at home in the society of farm laborers and the polite world.

Genuineness and modesty are the keys of friendship.

I Know

Volume 6

I know I can do as I please. At least I can always refuse. Hence I know that I am responsible for my actions. I will accept this responsibility and play the man. I will not be ever seeking excuses for my weakness.

I know I do not understand all the secret springs of the acts of others, hence I will be charitable in my judgments.

I know that what I know is to what I do not know as one is to infinity, hence I will try always to be teachable.

I know that the past cannot be changed, hence I will make the best of it; and that I cannot control the future, hence I will not worry about it.

I know that happiness depends more upon my thoughts than upon what happens to me, hence I will strive to control and adjust myself, instead of complaining of circumstances.

I know that the world is managed by a power and a will not of myself and greater than myself, hence I will try to understand and conform to it.

I know I cannot cheat nor evade the laws of nature, hence I will seek to find out what they are and obey them.

I know I have limitations, and that it is quite as important to understand them as it is to know my capacity.

I know that life is sweet to the healthy-minded, and therefore I will reject summarily any creed or opinion that degrades or mocks at life.

I know what love is. I do not always know what is right or wrong, nor what is wise or unwise. Therefore I can safely love everybody, and safely regulate nobody.

I know that suspicion is a disease of faith, jealousy is a disease of egotism, and envy is a disease of small natures; these I will avoid.

I know I can control and shape my tastes, my desires, and my thoughts, and I will not allow myself to be dominated by these.

I know that no sentiment, no feeling, is of value unless it enters into the will and is expressed in action.

I know that I will get from this world the equivalent only of what I give to it.

I know that, whatever God may be, a constant effort to do right is the only way to secure His approval. Whatever wrong I have committed, He becomes my friend when I begin to do right.

IDEALS

Everything is twofold. There is the thing itself, and there is the picture of the thing which is in the mind. That mental picture is called an Idea.

When we have a task we want to accomplish, a condition we want to attain, or any purpose at all, we form a mind-concept of the thing desired. That is called an Ideal.

When the architect builds a house he draws his plans which the workmen follow. The ideal is the soul's plan upon the trestle-board. Where there is no ideal, there is no development, no progress, no attainment, but the man drifts, and usually degenerates; just as the workmen without a disposing plan could make no house, but only a heap of stones.

When the orchestra plays it

follows the score of the composer. The ideal is the soul's score. Without it the soul is disordered, torn, and unhappy; just as there would be only wild discord if every musician in the orchestra played as he pleased without considering the others.

When the ship leaves port the captain knows where he wants to go. To the soul the ideal is as the ship's destination. Most people that never arrive fail because they have no goal. They sail aimlessly. They mistake motion for progress, and often the motion is in a circle.

Get an ideal. You do not succeed, because you do not know what you want, or you don't want it intensely enough.

Get an ideal. Determine upon what thing is most worthwhile to you in the whole world. Whether you reach that thing or not, the fact that you strike toward it, making every faculty, every deed and dream, bend toward one objective, will give symmetry, unity, and force to your personality.

Have an ideal of the kind of man you want to be, and try to express that in your everyday life.

Have an ideal of the position you want to occupy, and let every day's activities train you for that position.

Form an idea of the manners you would like to have, of the career you would choose, of the accomplishments you would find useful, of the language you would use, of the way you would conduct your business, fulfill your art, or demean yourself in your profession. Only so can you grow day by day and achieve contentment.

You may never reach your ideal; it may keep floating on and on before. But the sailor never reaches the North Star. Yet, without a north star he could never come to port.

IN PRAISE OF SORROW

Volume 2

To one who has brooded long over the mystery of this world and his own soul no law is more salient and strange than the efficiency of sorrow.

It is joy we all follow and praise and worship, but what a wastrel and ne'er-do-weel it is. We have laughed and danced and sung, but what has come of it? What indeed but certain mocking echoes, revealing the hollow emptiness of our prison of circumstance?

While, on the contrary, whatever substantial steps mankind has made have been by the crutches of pain.

'Tis the laborer sweating in the field that feeds the world, 'tis the soldier dying in battle that cures diseased governments, 'tis the workman reeling in the heat of the steel-mill or riveting girders at dizzy heights that builds our houses, 'tis the agonizing mother that brings forth the child, and the starving poet that furnishes our fancy.

What considerable value did we ever get from picnics? Was any scientific discovery, to bless mankind, ever thought out on a pleasure yacht? All the benefit to the human race that ever came from the piazzas of summer hotels, from cabarets and midnight frolics, from all games good or bad, from all hours of satiety or hilarity, you could put in your eye.

Only from the wounds and bruises of the world comes its healing. Only from its suffering comes its greatness. Only from its dark chambers of anguish emerge its abiding comforts and graces.

There was something of deep insight into the paradox of life that characterized the Puritan's grimness.

For cruelty is not far behind pleasure, lust is the child of lightness, and beneath the smooth surface of the sensualist lurks the horror of heartlessness.

By all means let us be happy when we may, but let us not falter at the door of sacrifice and pain, for only within the crypt of sorrow lie the rich and mystic treasures of the soul.

To suffer is to know life. Out of disappointment, disillusion, failure, humiliation, betrayal, bereavement, loneliness, out of such bitter moments come those supernal, transforming, ennobling qualities that sit like starry crowns upon us, and reveal us as sons of heaven.

That smile touches our hearts and wins us that is the ripple upon pensive deeps. The idiot mirth of the shallow saddens us.

Joy is good; let us seek it. But sorrow, which no man seeks, but which destiny thrusts on him, is better; let us not shun it.

Someone has said: "Joy impregnates; it is only sorrows that bring forth."

IRON IN THE SOUL

You need iron in your soul. Just as you need iron in your body.

And the best form in which to get iron is not any kind of iron tonic, pills, or tinctures, but such combinations of iron as occur in natural foods.

So you do not need any Spartan cult, any artificial toning up, under the spell of some fad, but daily iron that comes from right living.

What I mean by iron is that hardness of will, that rigidity of purpose, that firm self-mastery, which makes life strong and positive and efficient. To be more specific, what you need is a more virile will.

That means to have yourself so in hand that when your judgment says "I must," you obey gladly, without struggle or friction.

Most of our unhappiness comes from flabbiness of will. The will is clogged by desires. It moves laggardly, creakily, if at all.

The will ought to operate as tensely and promptly as a steel spring.

What a lot of plain and fancy misery we endure just because we cannot move swiftly to do the thing we ought—and enjoy it!

Men, women, and children are whining, puling, complaining, writhing, all because they have developed strong desires and no will to handle them.

How can I get iron into my soul's blood?

The first thing to do is to realize that the better and more permanent satisfactions of life are those we get by overcoming, not those we get by yielding.

Man is essentially a master. The ego is wretched when it is not dominant. And the first thing of all

to dominate is one's self.

Self-mastery is not the secret of power only, but also of joy.

The happy, cheerful, contented person is not the one that everlastingly "has strawberries, sugar, and cream, and sits on a cushion and sews a fine seam." No one ever got to heaven nor into a heavenly state of mind (permanently) by self-indulgence.

Discipline is the father of happiness.

Right on the heels of self-pampering, ever follow the seven devils of perversion, with their seven whips of pain, and their seven poisoned prods of self-contempt.

Then, having realized the need of self-mastery, you must practise it.

And do not take it up as an exercise apart from your life, like dumb-bells, but put it into your daily program. Plan to be daily at something that calls for coercing self. Do regularly something hard. William James used to say we ought to do every day two or three things we particularly disliked—just for practise.

Change your tastes—in work, in play, in eating, and drinking, in music, in art. Make up your mind what you OUGHT to like and drill yourself into liking it. Otherwise it's downstream for you.

Change your desires. Do not forever be led by the nose by your cravings.

Re-enthrone your intelligence, and put the sceptre of will in its hand.

The pits of wretchedness, world-weariness, and boredom are full of the slackers and weaklings. The drunkards, dope victims, sex perverts, loafers, and all the innumerable company of the lost, are they that have no iron in the soul.

IT TAKES GRIT

Volume 2

It takes grit to do anything worth doing. All real progress is upstream.

All the real crowns—soul-crowns and achievements crowns, not gold crowns—are rewards for fighting.

It takes grit—

To be patient,

To keep your temper,

To improve your mind,

To exercise, and keep your body fit,

To diet, that is, to eat for health and not for sport,

To save money,

To push your business,

To tell the truth,

To keep your mind clean, your mouth clean, and your soul clean,

To say no,

To do what you don't want to do, which means discipline,

To pay your debts,

To be loyal—to your ideals, to your wife, to your husband, to your friend, to your country,

To say, "I don't know,"

To do your own thinking,

To resist the mob,

To be honest, simple, and straight,

And not to worry.

But these things are easy:

To be irritable,

To give way to impulse, to say, "I can't help it," and to make no effort to control yourself,

To be mentally lazy, read nothing but trash, and have no habits of study,

To loaf, and to exercise only when you feel like it,

To eat what you please,

To wait for something to turn up,

To lie, to be disloyal, and to be unclean,

To agree with those you feel to be wrong, just to avoid trouble,

To side-step,

To go in debt, and to say, "Charge it!"

To join something and use partisanship for loyalty,

To go with the crowd,

To acquire a bad habit, and to nurse it along,

To follow your impulses and not your intelligence,

To fill your body with disease, your mind with error, and your soul with evil,

To slump, to pity yourself, to make excuses for yourself, to magnify your ego and ruin your character,

And to commit suicide.

It's easy going down.

It takes grit to go up, to get on, and even to keep decent.

IT WON'T WORK

It won't work, eh? You say it's all right to have ideals, but you've got to be practical in this world. Personal convictions are commendable, but in actual life one must trim, and accommodate, and compromise, to get along. It is well to be good and kind and generous, and to return good for evil, and turn the other cheek and all that, but really, you know, in this world one cannot possibly put such a program through. He would be eaten up.

So!

Yes, you continue, we must face facts. We must deal with stern realities. It is conditions that confront us, and not theories. We must live on earth, not among dreams.

Very well!

Let us stick to stubborn, hard, tough facts. Let us waste no time debating theories.

And let us ask:

1. Did you ever try the ideal life?

Did you ever honestly, for a fair space of time, long enough to get results, test the plan of absolute intellectual honesty, altruism, and the principle of the Beatitudes?

Answer: The most of you have not. You simply THINK it won't work. You BELIEVE that you would be imposed upon, wronged, and devoured. It is YOU who are the theorist.

As a matter of fact, the majority of people don't know whether living the higher, finer, ideal life will work or not. They have never tried it.

2. How many persons do you know who do consistently and persistently try it? Have you noted them carefully, if you have met any?

And if you have studied their cases, haven't you found that invariably they are cheerful, contented, happy, and strong in character?

Did it never occur to you, being

a practical soul, that all this commonly accepted talk of "be good and you'll be lonesome," and "the Ten Commandments and the Sermon on the Mount are iridescent dreams," is sheer dogmatism, pure speculation, and rests on no facts whatever?

And what facts you do use are isolated, spasmodic experiments in idealism you have made, or have heard that others have made, here and there, and not any settled habit of life.

3. Also take a look at your samples—there are plenty of them—who are trying the opposite program. The selfish, grasping, vindictive, vengeance-seeking, proud, shrewd, cunning, hard, cruel, pleasure-chasing crowd, eating and drinking to repletion, mad for new amusements, eager to be rich, famous, powerful—look at them, the world is full of them—are they full of the joy of life?

On the contrary, they are restless, unsatisfied, pessimistic, world-weary, bored, pitying their poor selves, and suspecting everybody else.

If you have so much "practical" common sense, why not use it? Why not get hold of a few facts and quit theorizing about something of which you have no actual knowledge?

It won't work, eh—to be good?

Perhaps not. Try it and see.

JAPANESE COMMON SENSE

Volume 3

Josh Billings once said something to the effect that experience was a good thing, but that the smart man would let the other fellow get bit by the rattlesnake while he took the experience.

Wisdom doubtless is excellent. But the trouble with it is that usually it is accumulated only after a long life, and by that time it's of not much use.

The time for wisdom is when you're young. Then you can utilize it to promote your success and ensure your happiness.

The first thing the young person wants to do is to decide that he wants wisdom, that he prefers being wise to being a fool.

This is difficult, for youth's passions are so strong, its delusions are so intense, and its impatience so great that it is an easy prey to the fakers that abound. He is persuaded by his own folly or by the talk of fools that wisdom means dullness and dryness, whereas in reality there is no great adventure, no abiding pleasure, and no real getting on without wisdom.

There are two sources from which he can get wisdom: from books, and from those who are old and wise.

To these he must add a strong and saving common sense, within himself, so that he may be able to judge, to discriminate between the true and the false, the seeming and the actual.

Yoritomo was one of Japan's most illustrious thinkers. He was founder of the first dynasty of Shoguns and ranked as one of the three greatest statesmen his country ever produced. He lived seven hundred years ago, but his teachings are evergreen.

He said that common sense is made up of various ingredients, of which five are reason, moderation, penetration, consistency, and wisdom.

Speaking of wisdom, he writes:

"It is from the never-ending lesson which life teaches us that wisdom of old age is learned.

"But is it really necessary to reach the point of decrepitude in order to profit by an experience? Why give to old age alone the privileges of wisdom? Why should its beauty be unveiled only to those who can no longer profit by it?

"What would be thought of one who prided himself on possessing bracelets when he had lost his two arms in war?

"It is, therefore, necessary not only to encourage young people to profit by lessons of wisdom and experience, but, still further, to indicate to them how they can accomplish the result of those lessons.

"To those who insist that nothing is equivalent to personal experience, we point out that a just opinion can only be formed when personal sentiment is excluded from the discussion.

"Is it necessary to have experienced pain in order to prevent or cure it?

"The majority of physicians have never been killed by the disease they treat.

"Then why could we not do for the mind that which can be done for the body?

"We may all possess wisdom if we are willing to be persuaded that the experience of others is as useful as our own."

Like almost everything else, self-confidence is a habit. It is formed by persistently choosing to let the mind dwell upon our successes, and in turning our thoughts just as persistently away from our failures.

—THE HABIT OF SELF-CONFIDENCE

JOB AND HIS WIFE

—————————————————————————————*Volume 5*

"Curse God and die!" exclaimed Job's wife when calamity piled upon him. "Though He slay me, yet will I trust Him," answered Job. And these two attitudes still characterize the world.

The woman reasoned that because her husband lost his flocks and houses, his children died, and boils came on him, therefore if there was a Providence it was a malicious one.

Something in Job's nature made him argue more deeply, clinging to his faith in the eternal goodness.

Today the issue is still fresh. When the young wife dies at the very time her husband and children need her most; when the —saint has a cancer and the drunken loafer remains in sound health; when the good and kind fall into poverty and the wicked wax fat and kick, there are those who jeer and say, "Where now is your good God, and what kind of a moral universe do you call this?"

Not long ago there appeared in the *Mercure of Paris* a most bitter arraignment of Divinity because [of] the present monstrous chaos of horror had been permitted in Europe. It expressed the query of many: "If it is the law of history that righteousness prospers and evil is punished, if the meek shall inherit the earth, and bloody men stumble on to ruin, why this hideous war?"

But Job's decision was the sounder. Maeterlinck has clearly put it in modern terms, in his *Wisdom and Destiny,* saying that the popular notion is superficial and mistakes entirely the grounds of ethical conviction.

For, he declares, our belief in morality arises not from the apparent justice of the universe, but from its apparent injustice.

If every good deed were straightway visibly rewarded and every bad deed immediately punished we should not believe in justice at all; we should all be slaves, unreasoning children, and time-servers.

We become moral only when we are thrown back upon our instincts by the seeming injustice of destiny.

Morality is not produced by any weighing of profit and loss, nor by rewards and punishments; morality is not a policy. It is not adopted by the shrewd and wise because it pays; it is believed in by the simple and heroic because it does not pay.

Morality is a result of faith, not intellect.

The man who sees how a good deed will profit him, and hence does it, is not moral; he is cunning. It is the man who does not see, yet does his good deed from inner compulsion, that is moral.

Prosperity was the reward of the Old Testament, said Bacon; adversity of the New.

You cannot lure men to grandeur of soul by sugarplums. To make men good you must appeal to the soldier feeling in them. When Garibaldi offered his ragged recruits wounds and hardships and death, and asked who now would follow him, the Italians cheered, threw their caps in the air, and volunteered in a frenzy of patriotism. You cannot arouse that kind of sentiment by promising gold and luxury.

It is not the tears of vile men but their prosperity and laughter here and now that makes us believe in the Day of Judgment.

The universe and its events do not make man moral; man makes the universe moral.

The throne of God is in the breast of mankind.

The rich and contented and smugly satisfied do not bother much about a Just Judge; it is those who, when cast down and bleeding, cry out, "Though He slay me, yet will I trust Him," that attain unto moral sublimity.

THE JOY OF WORK

Volume 8

The joy of doing one's work is the purest, least diluted, most permanent, divine, and abiding joy of which a human being is capable.

There are other joys that are fiercer, and with these our souls are lured into snares of pain.

The appetites have their pleasures, but behind every one of them stand the dark constables of sorrow. Behind the banquetter stand repletion and disease, gout and dyspepsia; behind the drinker's jovial hour stand folly and excess; behind the crowning moment of desire stand the Cossacks of disgust and remorse ready to charge; behind pride looms humiliation; behind riches the hollowness of luxury; and behind life itself, and its indulgences, death and the grave.

But behind work, rest; behind all good craftsmanship, unstained satisfaction; behind endeavor, heaven.

If work be a curse of Good inflicted upon mankind for the sin of our first parents, as some theologians have contended, then, as shrewder theologs have reasoned, the curse of God is better than the blessing of men.

But work is no punishment. On the contrary, it is the most redemptive of things.

He who loves work gains all the favors of the gods.

He gets health; for there is no purge nor tonic so efficient to the body as work.

He gets joy, for the most perfect joy of which we are capable is the forthputting of all one's powers.

He gets poise, for in loving labor is the true balance of all our faculties.

He gets dignity, for man never appears nobler than when he is glorified in his work. He gets praise, for the only commendation that does not make us feel sheepish is that bestowed upon us for good work.

He gets fellowships, for there is no companionship so pure and wholesome as that of those who work together at some worthy business.

He gets self-respect, for there is no satisfaction so unalloyed as the consciousness of having done well that which we have undertaken to do.

He gets rest, for work alone brings rest in all its grateful sweetness, such as the idler in his restive hours of inaction cannot understand.

He gets goodness, for it is doubtful if any virtue at all can be held unspoiled by those whose souls are thrown into no task.

He gets faith, for all belief in the eternal laws of goodness comes from the doers, and all doubt and despair from the triflers and undoers.

So for heaven I imagine no place of everlasting rest, but of eternal youthfulness in labor where "no one shall work for money, and no one shall work for fame."

Neither do I fancy it as a triumph. For human blessedness is not found in success, but in effort; not in arriving, but in travelling; not in the wages and guerdons of work, but in work itself.

Therefore heaven seems to me as the place

"Where human power and failure
Are equalized forever,
And the great light that haloes all
Is the passionate bright endeavor."

JUST RIGHT

Volume 2

There is a certain point at which anything is just right: not enough is bad, too much is worse.

The good cook browns the roast to a turn.

The wise mother rebukes and praises just to the right degree.

The good wife is not too cold, not too loving—she's just right.

The good friend knows how to compliment us just "to the saturation-point."

The good tragedian is just tragic enough, and the good comedian not too funny.

There is just one exact place on the violin-string where you must put your finger in order to produce the perfect tone.

Don't speak too low or you will be a nuisance because you will annoy those who try to hear you; and if you speak too loudly you will also be a nuisance, for another reason.

The art of life is to eat, drink, laugh, cry, work and play, love and hate—just right.

I read somewhere the happy phrase: "He was dressed more like a gentleman than a gentleman ought to dress."

JUSTICE

Volume 10

There are many earnest souls occupied in trying to do people good.

There are nine million societies, more or less, organized to improve and to ameliorate.

There are preachers, missionaries, evangelists, reformers, exhorters, viewers-with-pride, and pointers-with-alarm without number wrestling with sinners.

All forms of industry are booming these days in the USA, but the uplift business is still several laps ahead.

It seems ungracious to say a word to any enthusiastic person who is engaged in so laudable an enterprise as that of rescuing the perishing, feeding the hungry, and healing the sick.

And yet, when you take time to think right through to the bottom of things, you must come to the conclusion that there is but one real, radical and effective way to help your fellow-men, and that is the way called justice.

If I want to redeem the world I can come nearer my object, and do less harm, by being just toward myself and just toward everybody else, than by "doing good" to people.

The only untainted charity is justice.

Often our ostensible charities serve but to obscure and palliate great evils.

Conventional charity drops pennies in the beggar's cup, carries bread to the starving, distributes clothing to the naked. Real charity, which is justice, sets about removing the conditions that make beggary, starvation, and nakedness.

Conventional charity plays Lady

Bountiful; justice tries to establish such laws as shall give employment to all, so that they need no bounty.

Charity makes the Old Man of the Sea feed sugarplums to the poor devil he is riding and choking; justice would make him get off his victim's back.

Conventional charity piously accepts things as they are, and helps the unfortunate; justice goes to the legislature and changes things.

Charity swats the fly; justice takes away the dung-heaps that breed flies.

Charity gives quinine in the malarial tropics; justice drains the swamps.

Charity sends surgeons and ambulances and trained nurses to the war; justice struggles to secure that internationalism that will prevent war.

Charity works among slum wrecks; justice dreams and plans that there be no more slums.

Charity scrapes the soil's surface; justice subsoils.

Charity is affected by symptoms; justice by causes.

Charity assumes evil institutions and customs to be a part of "Divine Providence," and tearfully works away at taking care of the wreckage; justice regards injustice everywhere, custom-buttressed and respectable or not, as the work of the devil, and vigorously attacks it.

Charity is timid and is always passing the collection-box; justice is unafraid and asks no alms, no patrons, no benevolent support.

"It is presumed," says Henry Seton Merriman, "that the majority of people are willing enough to seek the happiness of others; which desire leads the individual to interfere with his neighbor's affairs, while it burdens society with a thousand associations for the welfare of mankind or the raising of the masses."

The best part of the human race does not want help, nor favor, nor charity; it wants a fair chance and a square deal.

Charity is man's kindness. Justice is God's.

KEEP YOUR CHIN UP

Volume 3

I am going to tell you the truth about this naughty world, and the truth is that whichever way you're going, up or down, people want to help you along.

If you are going up we all want to boost; if you are going down we all want to push. That is what we call sympathy.

You hear complaints that the rich are growing richer and the poor poorer. That has always been the case, simply because it is human nature. Society has always been organized to increase the wealth of the wealthy and the power of the powerful; also to make the weak weaker.

The rule is that "to him that hath shall be given, and from him that hath not shall be taken away even that which he hath."

There's no use whining about it. It is simply one of the flinty laws of nature. The only thing to do with nature's laws is to adjust one's self to them and not to complain.

This might be called the law of the inertia of prosperity.

You are guilty yourself. Whom do you want to see? The man everybody wants to see. And you read the book everybody's reading, and go to the store where it is "the thing" to go.

"Follow the crowds," says the advertiser, with his shrewd knowledge of our make-up. If you have a hundred dollars ahead, to whom do you want to hand it? To the poor man who needs it? Not at all, but to the rich banker who does not need it.

If I ask you for the loan of a quarter you will pass it over to me without a word if you think it is a trifling matter to me; but if you suspect I really am in want, and need the quarter to buy a little food with, that's quite another affair; you can't encourage that sort of thing; I should go to the Associated Charities.

Now, the way to use this law is to feign prosperity even if you have it not. Keep your chin up.

Wear good clothes. Don't withdraw from the society of the prosperous. Look pleasant. Don't let yourself get down at the heel. Don't get that poor beggar look on your face.

It isn't hypocrisy. It isn't pretense. It is sheer courage. It is letting the world know that while you live you purpose to fight, and that like old General Taylor you "don't know when you're licked."

Keep smiling and an unfriendly universe will not know what to do with you; so it will crown you.

Says Alfred de Vigny: "All those that struggle against the unjust heavens have had the admiration and secret love of men."

Fate is a bluff. Face her, defy her, and she will fawn on you.

Fate is cruel, but only to the quitter.

Fear is the greatest enemy to the human soul.
—The Greatest Enemy

KEEP YOUR MIND

——————————————————————————————*Volume 9*

Keep. That is the main word in this article. So look at it, spell it, repeat it, feel of it, say it, chew it, swallow it, and digest it.

Don't you ever take one word and turn it over and over in your mind, finding new significances, connotations, adumbrations, and echoes in it?

Looking up its etymology in the dictionary we find that *keep* has just come down to us plump from the old Anglo-Saxon. It means nothing but *keep,* and always has meant just that. It's a comfort to find a word once in a while whose ancestry has not wobbled.

Of all keepings the best is to keep your mind.

That, of course, does not mean not to let anyone take it away from you, but to defend it, to maintain its integrity, to preserve it against attacks that would weaken it or unbalance it, or loosen or dilute it.

The greatest enemy that threatens is fear. Fear paralyzes or arouses destructive activities. It is the great enemy of sanity. Our chief struggle is to keep fear out.

Fear has many fellows, such as premonitions, suspicions, ignorance, and the like.

The mind is a river; upon its water thoughts float through in a constant procession every conscious moment. It is a narrow river, however, and you stand on a bridge over it and can stop and turn back any thought that comes along, and they can come only single file, one at a time. The art of contentment is to let no thought pass that is going to disturb you.

Keep your mind.

Keep it as an inner citadel of peace.

Then you can sleep. Insomnia is due to letting upsetting Bolshevik thoughts pass in and start trouble.

Outside the inner ring of quiet and common sense is a fringe of ugly and bandit thoughts always ready to break in, a fringe of horror and panic and distress. Keep your mind. Let not the evil enter.

Disturbing suggestions are constantly being shot as arrows at you. Look to your shield. Keep your mind.

Jinx thoughts, spook thoughts, bugaboo thoughts, goblin thoughts, bad luck thoughts, devil thoughts, are always flying in the air like mosquitoes. Look to your screens. Keep your mind.

If a matter causes you uneasiness face it, think it out, decide upon the best course of action—and forget it.

Don't say you cannot. You can do a deal more with thoughts than you suppose. You can manage them, drive them away, dodge them, invite them and otherwise master and manipulate them.

But to do this requires two things. First, that you believe you can do it. And second, practise.

You achieve the ability to keep your mind as you learn to play the violin; that is, by wanting to do it, by studying, and by infinite practise.

But the result is worth the effort.

LAYING UP

The thrifty man lays up money for his old age. The farmer lays up fodder for his winter feeding. The medical student lays up information for use in his future practise. The intelligent, by due exercise and diet, lay up health, and the wastrel lays up trouble and disease by his excesses.

All of us lay up something, willy-nilly.

It is a good idea to ask one's self, in considering any act we are about to perform, not only what will be the immediate pleasure in it, but what sort of product we are laying up for ourselves by it.

We are always coming into our inheritance from our past deeds.

Maeterlinck says, "There is one thing that can never turn into suffering, and that is the good we have done."

This day you may have to decide between doing a thing that will gain you a thousand dollars and a

thing that will cost you ten. In making up your mind it is well to take into consideration what happiness dividend the transaction is going to bring you ten years from now.

The world you live in is formed on the laying-up principle. Nature gains her ends as a child learns to walk and talk, by infinite repetitions. She does the same thing over and over. She is eternally learning how.

Think how many centuries she practised in fish-flappers, bird-wings, and animal fore-legs, until she could make a human arm.

Let the scientist tell you of the infinite trials that preceded the formation of an eye, an ear, a human brain.

The efficiency of every age depends upon what was laid up for it by the ages gone before. This age of coal and petroleum rests upon the long cycles of the carboniferous era, when summer after summer giant trees grew and fell, and in the crucible of earth were changed to coal and oil!

Nature never forgets. She never drops a stitch. What she does now is a part of what she has in mind for ten thousand years from now. The plan of the oak is in the acorn.

"The books were opened," says the Apocalypse, describing the Day of Judgment, "and the dead were judged out of the things that were written in the books." This parable is but a picture of the scientist's declaration that our EVERY ACT LEAVES ITS RUT IN THE BRAIN, making us prone to repeat; what we feel today we more readily feel tomorrow; every functioning of body or mind, in fact, having memory-making as a by-product. The whole process looks toward a future man.

Creation is cumulative. That is the meaning of evolution.

The human race is cumulative. That we learn from reading history.

The individual life is cumulative. Every day is for future days. Every sensation and every act of will, everything I do, has a bearing upon the me that shall be ten years from this time—a thousand, a million years hence—who knows?

Hence, if anyone chooses to believe that, after this long getting-ready, Nature is going to throw me, body and soul, back into the scrap-heap, let him believe it.

Nature ought to have as much sense as I have. And I certainly would not go to all the pains Nature takes in preparing a human spirit only to fling my product at last into the ditch.

LIBERTY

Volume 5

There is nothing so needful as liberty, and nothing that needs to be more clearly understood.

After all, the real freedom life craves is freedom to choose its own masters.

When I say I want to be free to love, I mean that I want to be free to become a slave, for love is neither sweet nor true except it be a bondage. The lover does not want to be unchained. Freedom—from her—would be horrible.

Free love is a contradiction of terms. It is not love unless it binds me irresistibly.

How deep is the error men fall into when they do not see this!

Free-thought, when it is a revolt against conviction, is absurd; it is only worthy when it means freedom to obey abjectly what seems to be the truth.

Freedom in religion really means the right to follow my own religion, and not the absence of any reverence.

Freedom, then, does not signify the absence of restraint; truth and love are both essentially absolute czars. Freedom signifies simply that you shall not put your restraints upon me.

For some people seem to agree with the Abbe Galiani: "Liberty is the right to meddle with the affairs of others."

LIFE AS A BUSINESS PROPOSITION

Life has been called all sorts of things. Life is a dream, a gambling game, an opportunity from which to get all the fun and the least pain possible, a probation preparatory to the next life, a vale of tears, and so on.

Suppose we consider life as a business proposition. Look at it from a practical, profit-and-loss, shrewd, and commonsense viewpoint.

Very well. First, what can we get out of it? Only wages. There are no endowed and privileged ones, all are day laborers; for every one, when the work's over, must leave all he has gained and go back to that nothingness from which he came, as stark naked and poor as when he arrived. All the billionaire gets out of life is exactly what the bricklayer gets, his board and clothes and amusements.

What is the wage of life? Life's pay is happiness. On life's book happiness is credit and unhappiness debit.

It's happiness we all strive for, of one kind or another, whether beer and cakes or turtled feasts, overalls or dress-suits, pinochle on a cracker-box or stock-gambling on the market, social distinction, wealth display, political success, intellectual achievement—it's all happiness, according to taste.

How is happiness to be secured; how can one be sure to get his pay? By finding out what he really wants. This is not so easy. Most people work a lot for what they think other people think they want.

How can one find that out? By experiment, trying out various activities until he finds the one in which he can most enthusiastically express himself.

Also by ascertaining those forms of pleasure that are frauds and bring on misery. The conclusive argument against drunkenness, licentiousness, and the like, is that they are swindles, gold bricks; they promise joy and pay suffering.

How should one get his pay? Every day. Not at the end of the task. Unless every day brings its satisfaction, you are cheating yourself.

How can one tell what sort of things pay and what sort do not pay? By the collective experience of mankind, and by accepting the guidance of reliable teachers.

What does the cumulative experience of mankind show? That only those acts which are fundamentally just, fair, honest, and kind are those that invariably pay.

What's the good of morality? Morals rest not upon authority, but are the massed wisdom of the world. The person who is not moral is a fool, which is worse than being a sinner. He is a lamb, a sucker, a greenhorn, fully as much as a country-jake who thinks he can beat the Wall Streets experts. Immorality means docking the happiness pay-envelope every day.

Of what practical value are the higher sentiments? If you are helpful, unselfish, courteous, patient, reverent, loyal, just, and benevolent, you get a large bonus daily in your happiness pay.

Are not crafty, selfish, unclean, cruel, and conscienceless people happy? Get right well acquainted with them and see. They are the bunco-steeres, the confidence-men, the criminal cheats of life. Their books are false. Their happiness profits are worthless paper.

Why work? If it's happiness that is our wage, why not eat, drink, and be merry; why not loaf and play? Because human beings are so constituted that they secure the maximum of satisfactory self-expression only by doing some part of the world's work.

Why study to improve the mind, or to develop one's spiritual capacities? Why not go in for all the fun we can get each day? Because, by increasing our mental and spiritual powers, we get the more permanent, the higher, and rarer forms of happiness—we get gold and not copper.

What we call goodness more than pays every day; it leaves something over, a deposit in the happiness bank, which becomes a reserve fund from which we draw dividends. The good are the happiness capitalists. The bad are the happiness spendthrifts.

Why not approach this matter of good and bad, conscience or self-indulgence, as a business proposition?

No soul can be lost by anything the world can do
to it; only by what it can do to itself.

—WHAT IS A LOST SOUL?

LIGHT AND BURNING

Behind every glow is a burning. Behind every light is heat.

And behind all helpful influence is sacrifice.

The sun's light is gentle and life-giving; we bask in its rays, the little flowers look up and love it, and the green earth rejoices. Yet behind the wide and welcome glow, at the central spot whence emanates this comfortable and mothering sheen, there are what roaring flames, boilings of molten rock, cataclysmic and violent fires!

So the secret of influence is sacrifice. What good you do is measured by how much you are burning. The power of your love ray is in proportion to the conflagration within your heart.

The painter is great when he dips his brush in the fountain of his blood.

The author lays his compelling mind upon the lives of thousands when he has written by the light of his own soul-burning.

The actor touches you when he pours out his life into his role.

Mothers are great because they consume their lives so fully for their children.

Peace, comfort, progress, civilization—somebody must keep up the fires for these.

This so great America, with its rushing trains, humming factories, fruitful farms, busy schools, offices, and markets, what is it but the bright light caused by the burning up of human souls, labor, the consumption of lives?

And in heaven, it is said, "the Lamb is the light thereof." For all the beauty and bliss of the place is but the radiance of the great sacrifice.

The spirit of the man is the candle of the Lord, is the saying. It sends out light and power only when it burns.

There is a deeper analogy than we suspect in Shakespeare's couplet:

> "How far that little candle throws
> its beams!
> So shines a good deed in a naughty
> world."

Anger is sometimes unavoidable, as when we witness or hear of some outrageous act of injustice or cruelty. But if we must have it, let it be quick and soon over. For when it remains in us it is we who suffer, and not our adversary.

—ANGER POISON

THE LIMITATIONS OF SCIENCE

Volume 4

Science has done wonders, but it has its limitations.

In the days when Huxley and Tyndall were in their prime there was a feeling in the air that science was a new omnipotence that was about to solve all problems, cure all social ills, dispel all clouds of superstition, and bring the sunlight of truth and gladness of light upon earth.

The reaction could not fail to come. We have learned that science, too, is human.

The world is under an unpayable debt to the scientific spirit and the scientific method. They have done great things.

But there are other things, and the greatest things of all, that science cannot do.

For, after all, the eye of the scientist sees only appearances. The eye of the microscope, as a recent French essayist has said, is still only an eye, and sees only appearances.

Science recognizes only facts. But it is not facts that have the last word in life—it is the relations of human beings to those facts.

So it is always to the "seer," to the poet and prophet, the philosopher and the storyteller, that we must turn for our last adjustment.

When our facts are non-facts, when we base our preachment upon what is not true, of course we go astray. It is science that must lay our foundations, else the house is built on the sand and will not stand.

But science has been over-praised. It has made racing locomotives, huge steamships, telegraphic cables, and telephones. With these we have saved time and money, but we are no nearer the solution of the problem of what we shall do with the spare time we have gained or the excess wealth we have piled up.

Science has brought forth millionaires; it has not brought forth any word to make them a blessing and not a burden to the world.

It has enabled us to carry bodies ten times faster than in the age of Moses; it has not shown how to make the souls in those bodies nobler.

Is the mystery of love any clearer now than it was in the days of Abelard and Heloise?

Is death more understandable to the last mother who lost her baby than it was to Eve, sitting with dead Abel's head in her lap?

Are there modern formulas of friendship more reliable than the instincts of Damon and Pythias?

Can the most learned savant of Harvard or the Sorbonne tell you anything new about how to starve the beast and nourish the angel in you, anything Marcus Aurelius or Paul of Tarsus had not told?

Has the most distinguished professor of sociology given us any new light on how human beings are to live in mutual helpfulness and peace, any light that goes beyond the beams cast by the pure ideals of Jesus of Nazareth?

Let us honor the scientist. He has abolished pests, increased comforts, banished the ghosts of ignorance, and taught us intellectual honesty.

But he has not healed the deep hurt of the world, and he never can. That takes another type of man.

LITTLES

Volume 7

What people think of you usually depends on little things, but what people think of you is no little thing.

Hence, son, incline your ear unto me, and I will give you some intimate hints; they are littles, but you would do well to read, mark, learn, and inwardly digest them.

As to your clothes, wear just what is expected of one in your circumstances. The height of good dressing is not to be noticed. Whatever tends to attract attention is on the way to vulgarity.

Cultivate cleanliness. Keep your clothing clean, your skin clean, your nails clean, your teeth clean.

Avoid marked perfumes. The best perfume in the world is the kind that suggests soap; the worst, the kind that suggest you forgot the soap. And eschew jewelry.

Choose your crowd. Don't go with those who spend more than you can afford, drink what you don't want to drink, or talk the way you don't like. Don't criticize. Just drop out.

Don't be officious. Don't qualify in the popular art of minding other people's business. Don't regulate.

Be gentle. The stronger the gentler. The more power you have, use it the more carefully.

Don't bluff. If you are going to hit a man, hit him and have done with it.

Don't hold a grudge. If the man is mean, it's too great a compliment to him to waste time and vitality hating him.

Train your voice. Speak low. When you see you are losing your temper, if you drop your voice about a third you will find you will regain command of yourself. Don't mumble. Pronounce the consonants. Finish your sentences.

Don't argue. Discuss. The difference is, that in argument you are trying to outdo the other fellow; in discussion you are trying to get at the truth.

Be courteous. Practise at home. Get up when your wife enters the room. Be polite to your baby. Then it will come easier when you want to show off. Learn how to converse. One way is to be interested in what the other person is saying, instead of thinking, all the time he is talking, of what you are going to say when he is done.

Don't talk about yourself. Don't talk of your disease, your family, your babies, your servants, your troubles, your successes. Listen to Jones talk of his. That will make a hit with Jones. And what do you care?

Don't interrupt. Wait till the other person runs down before you begin to speak.

In general discussion be the last to speak. Then you can utter the veriest platitude and it will sound grand.

The easiest way to get a reputation for being deep is to keep still. "Even a fool is counted wise when he holdeth his peace," said Solomon.

Break yourself of any unpleasant mannerisms, such as twisting your mouth, toying with your mustache, working with your eyebrows, twirling your thumbs, posing or squirming, or drumming with your fingers.

All these things obstruct and belie your personality. And the art of pleasing consists in perfectly expressing yourself, simply, naturally, and with ease.

LIVING VERSUS PASSING THE TIME

Volume 5

A certain prefect, banished by Vespasian, left Rome to finish his days in the country; it was he who said:

"I have passed sixty and ten years upon the earth, and I have lived seven of them," alluding to the profitable time he had spent in the country, cultivating his garden and his soul, as compared with the tumultuous nonexistence at the capital.

Here is indicated a striking and thought-compelling comparison.

How much of your life have you lived, and how much of it have you merely passed?

Yesterday, for instance, did you live really? Or was it merely an interval between things regretted in the past and things hoped for in the future?

How often dare you say: "This now is life. I am happy. I am feeling the joy of existence. I am expressing my inner self completely"?

Or is your life always a tomor-row and tomorrow and tomorrow, with here and there bitter dashes of yesterday?

THE LYING ART OF MORBIDITY

Volume 1

Zola, Maupassant, Sudermann, D'Annunzio, Gorki, Tolstoy, and whoever else has written of life as a gloom, a groan, a tragedy, and a defeat are wrong. They are just as wrong now as the hermits and starving anchorites were wrong a thousand years ago. I do not criti-cize their literary excellence, nor say that they do not contain some truth, but the morbid cast they fling upon life is false, as everything sickly is false.

Life is healthy, fecund, full of juices and joys. Every spring with its burst of bloom and leaf-age, every child shouting at play in the street, every pair of lov-ers hand in hand in the moon-shine, every full-hearted mother among her babies, every hearty old man sitting in the sun, every bird dashing from tree to house-top singing, all these, the hum and flash and fragrance of life's throbbing dynamics, give the lie to crazy sorrow.

It is a lying art that makes death, a moment's pang, stain the white tissue of all one's days. Life is good, sweet, rich, and strong. We feel it in sunny Shakespeare, sanest of all lords of letters. Health, and not dis-ease, is the truth.

The "grand, gloomy, and pecu-liar" soul is perilously near a hum-bug. Please, God, I will live my years with my face to the light, meeting the blows of fate with a joke, the contempt of men with a smile, the plague and mystery of the unknown in my own heart and in the universe with cheerful faith, and death the best I can when I come as Maeter-linck implies when he makes old Arkel say, in *Pelleas and Melisande,* "Si j'etais Dieu j'aurais pitie des hommes"—If I were God I would have pity upon men.

And the third quality of the re-ligion of men of letters is courage. They seem to see the race of men as travellers from an unknown to an unknown country, played upon by strange forces, ruled by inscru-table fates, yet finding their joy not in slavish fear but in a brave domi-nance; for the tragedies that crush the petty do but liberate and en-noble the great.

And surely any soul, of whatever creed or of whatever unfaith, can but be enlarged and satisfied by joining in the appreciation of truth, of pity, and of courage, the religion of men of letters.

LYING TO YOURSELF

Volume 5

The private diary of Leo Tolstoy was recently published in Paris by his daughter, the Countess Alexandria Ivovna. One of his views therein expressed is:

"Lying to others is much less serious than lying to yourself."

To know this is the beginning of wisdom.

Self-deception is the starting-point of moral decay.

Lying to others may be but a harmless amusement, but lying to yourself is sure to mean inward deformity, the germ-laden fleck that spreads disease throughout your whole character.

Yet it is the commonest, easiest, most subtle of sins.

If you talk with the inmates of the penitentiary, with the crime-wrecked and drug-soaked of the slums, you will find that every one of them is living like a spider in a web of delusions he has woven out of his own substance.

The profligate has told himself that "the world owes him a living" until he believes it.

The criminal lays his downfall at the door of society.

The prostitute can glibly prove that she is not to blame, she is the victim of injustice.

Every down-and-outer labors to justify himself and trace his misfortune to others.

As a matter of fact, no person since the world began was ever compelled to do wrong.

No rotten stone or cracked beam was ever laid in the edifice of any man's character that he did not put there with his own hands.

When I say that another made me do an evil thing I lie to myself.

Others may have threatened, cajoled, tempted, pushed, or bribed me, but the fatal final step was never taken except by the consent of my own will.

You may offer me a habit-forming drug, you may argue with me that it will do me good, you may urge me by ridicule, and lead me on by example; and my appetite may second your efforts. I may crave the glass, my nerves may clamor for it, and my imagination may lure me to it; BUT I DO NOT HAVE TO DRINK.

Whatever excuses I may give, there is one thing I do not have to do, and I do only because I will do it, and that is to swallow the stuff.

And that is true of every injurious deed. If I do an act of fraud, or uncleanness, or cruelty, there is just one person guilty—it is myself.

The world is full of blubbering whiners, whimperers, and weaklings. Overfull.

That we do wrong is not so disgusting. We are all human, and perhaps all a little perverted. But having erred, let us be downright and manly and honest about it. Let us acknowledge our guilt, admit that our lusts and greeds and selfishness, which other people or circumstances may have deftly played upon, are no valid excuse, and that the responsibility for our evil rests absolutely upon ourselves. We may be sinners; but at least we can play the man.

Don't lie to yourself. Don't wallow in self-pity. Don't hunt extenuating circumstances. Don't justify yourself by comparing your own with others' wrongdoing.

The wickedness of others may bring pain or loss to you, through no fault of yours. Each of us must bear a portion of the vicarious burden of the world's evil. But mark this: you never did wrong for any other reason than that you chose to do it.

Not to have committed the wrong deed may have meant suffering to you or to those you love, may have meant humiliation, or calamity, or even death. BUT YOU DIDN'T HAVE TO DO IT. You could have died. You may have to suffer, to be humiliated, to endure tragedy, to die; nor you, nor any human being, ever had to do wrong.

So don't lie to yourself.

Honesty toward yourself is the key that will open to you the New Life.

THE MANNER OF GREATNESS

Volume 1

To act a vice or a virtue is to induce it. This is a well-known psychological law. Act petulant, you become petulant. Act the gentleman, and you get to feeling like a gentleman. Put on brutal manners and indulge in brutal words, and before long you are brutal.

The utility of this law is apparent when we become conscious of our shortcomings and want to improve ourselves. For instance, if

I am awkward and diffident I take the elegant Mr. Brummel for my model, I ape his ways, his voice, his carriage, and by and by I grow to be Brummelish in my mind. If I put on and wear a virtue or a vice long enough, I absorb it into my soul.

All this is a prelude to this point: that worry is the manifestation of weakness, and poise is the manner of power.

If I want power, therefore, and have it not, let me put away worry and put on poise, and power will come to me.

This is illustrated in the case of that figure which has been most conspicuous in American affairs, General Pershing.

"During the period when there was misunderstanding and miscarriage in the censorship," writes Charles H. Grasty, a correspondent of the American Press, "I had frequent occasion to talk to General Pershing and express my sense of grievance. He encouraged me to do so. One day I said to him:

" 'General, you have enough responsibilities. I am not going to worry you any more with faultfinding about the censorship.'

" 'Well, if you are letting that idea trouble you, dismiss it,' he replied with a smile. 'I don't let anything worry me. I try to do a good day's work, and when it is finished I go to bed. And what is more, I go to sleep.'"

Surely, what is good gospel for the man who stands in the "doubtful ridges of the battle" is good enough for you and me, in our small corner, isn't it?

Come, let us put on this man's excellence, though we have it not; let us practise the virtue we admire, and perhaps some of its quality may sink into us.

Just do our work "by the day"! Just do the best we can in all good conscience and leave the results in the lap of the gods! To make of difficulty the stuff of opportunity, and of confusion and danger the reason for self-mastery; to resist complaint as the mark of weakness, and worry as a sign of petty spirit; to do our bit in faithfulness, and "having done all, to stand"—this is the manner of power.

The brave, grim, cheerful American soldier ought to be a tonic to all of us.

Sin is personal. It lies not in the infraction of any code or rules, but in our inward cowardice and moral flabbiness, in our disloyalty to our own conviction, in our refusal to follow our sense of Ought.

—Sin

MANNERS

Your manner has a deal to do with your success.

Your manners are the printed page on which people read of what you are inside.

So what's the use of being grand and noble in your thought, intent, and purpose if the whole story is twisted, botched, and lied about by your way of expressing yourself?

People are usually very sensitive, very stupid, and very silly on the matter of improving their ways. They resent it when they are told to talk differently, to sit, walk, or stand in a better style.

You are apt to say: "I am what I am. If people don't like me I can't help it. I am as God made me."

But you are not. You are as circumstances, environment, and your own ignorance have spoiled you.

If you have a friend—an enemy is even better—who dares tell you the truth, go to him, and listen, and think over what he says.

When anyone criticizes you, or when you hear something disagreeable said of you, don't repel it with anger, but study over it, find out if it has a basis of truth, and improve yourself. Don't defend; reform.

Why should you let an unfortunate mannerism cling to you all your life, just because you are too lazy or too proud to rid yourself of it?

Do you walk lumberingly? Do you sit awkwardly? Have you got into the way of scowling habitually? Is your voice harsh and unpleasant, or loud, or shrill? Do you mumble your words?

You can change all these things and remove the disagreeable spot that is hurting you more than any one else if (1) you will acknowledge and see your weakness, and (2) if you will steadily practise to overcome.

Don't be a conceited fool. Don't make your objectionable qualities a part of your personality, which you feel called on always to defend.

One way to success is to get the manner of success.

Find someone whom you admire, someone who has poise and dignity and ease and is just about the sort of person you wish you were. Study him. Imitate him. Copy his little ways.

It's these little things that count. It makes a lot of difference how you speak, whether your words are coarse, inaccurate, and provincial or not.

Have courage to quit slouching, to learn how to sit correctly, to eat like a person of breeding, to quit screwing your mouth about, and laughing like a horse, and asking the price of your host's dishes, and blowing your nose like a trumpet, and using such words as *humanitarian* and *enthuse* and all such things.

Usually it is carelessness more than ignorance.

THE MEN WHO MAKE GOOD

—*Volume 3*

We are full of hidden forces. In a crisis we discover powers in ourselves, powers that have lain dormant, secret reserves of ability, only waiting [for an] occasion to leap forth.

You can tell just what strain a bar of iron will bear, just what weight a locomotive will pull, and just how much liquid a glass vessel will hold; but you cannot tell how much responsibility a man can carry without stumbling, nor how much grief a woman's heart can suffer without breaking.

The human being is the X in the problem of nature. He is the unknown quantity in the universe.

The frightened boy can jump a fence he would not attempt in his sober senses. A frail woman in the desire to save her child becomes as strong as Sandow. A soldier battle-mad acquires the strength of ten.

The one thing nobody knows is what he can do in a pinch.

The forceful natures are those that depend upon this hidden nerve force. These are the pioneers, to whom the danger from unknown beasts and savages is a welcome fillip. They taste

"That stern joy that warriors feel
In foeman worthy of their steel."

These are they that love "the doubtful ridges of the battle," that go down to the sea in ships, sing in the face of the storm, and laugh at the arrows of the sleet.

These are the overcomers.

These are the salt of the race.

These are the born kings of men—Carlyle's can-sing, cun-ning, king men, the men who can.

They do not know what they can do. They only know that when the thing is to be done, possible or impossible, safe or deadly, there is some strength that surges up within them that meets and measures with the task.

Panic only calms them, clears their brain, and steadies their hand while other men go mad.

Defeat only rouses in them a dogged strength.

Slander, sneers, and curses cannot drive them from their work; success or praise does not make them dizzy.

They are not prudent, they are not wise; they are not skilled and trained; they simply make good wherever they are put.

There is no recipe for producing such souls. The choicest heredity cannot breed them, schools cannot prepare them, religion cannot form them.

They are the men who rise to the occasion. They are the unafraid. They are those who lose themselves in the thing to be done, and do it, and care not for heaven or hell or for their own life.

The supply of such has never equalled the demand. Every business enterprise wants them, every profession cries for them.

They are not heroes. They are better; they are men.

When you meet them they seem commonplace, often shy and awkward.

But don't be deceived. They are the only really great men. For they are the men who make good.

THE MORNING STAR

Volume 8

Every man's career is a continued struggle of the two natures in us, the angel and the brute. Everybody is more or less a Dr. Jekyll and Mr. Hyde.

There may be some rare natures, such as Charles Kingsley calls "natural kingdom-of-heavenites," who always want to do the thing they ought to do, but they are scarce indeed.

The first thing to do, therefore, is to recognize that all decent life must be in terms of conflict. Because you feel this unceasing war within you is no sign that you are "bad," or selfish, or meaner than other people. You are simply human. You might as well complain that you do not have three hands, or that you do not possess supernatural powers of vision or hearing, as to complain that your inclination does not always agree with your duty.

Having recognized this fact, don't worry over it. Don't grow morbid. Don't call yourself names. Don't develop self-contempt. And above all, don't get into the mire of self-pity.

It's a fight. You have to make it. Go to it gayly, with high courage, and with gladness that you are disposed to fight and sure to win.

You can dodge the fight by yielding to your lower nature. As Oscar Wilde said, "The easiest way to get rid of temptation is to yield." But you know the nasty side to that. It means a weak, flabby, unclean mind, a spirit that must loathe itself.

But you can be just as comfortable as the sensualist if you make up your mind that you will do what is right every time, no matter how you feel. That will not give you the same kind of pleasure that the self-indulgent have, but a better kind.

For there are two sorts of enjoyment: one, that of yielding; the other, that of overcoming. And it is the overcomer that gets the crown of life. His is the morning star.

For instance, there is pleasure in lying in bed, in eating and drinking, in gratifying the various cravings of the body, in reading books that divert you and require no mental effort, in going to the theatre, in being flattered, praised, complimented, loved. In all these things your pleasure is passive.

There is pleasure, on the other hand, in exercise, in going without food and drink for another's sake, in denying the body's demands so as to satisfy the wants of your intelligence, of pleasing your conscience by trampling on an appetite, of intellectual exertion, of discipline, and the like.

All these are the solider kind of joys. They are better than the soft kind, because they last longer, they strengthen your mind and body, they make your tastes finer, your whole enjoyment of life keener, your range of delights wider, and altogether you get a deal more fun out of living.

The latter joys are just as "selfish" as the former. But an intelligent selfishness is unselfish. He that saveth his life shall lose it.

Scientifically speaking, overcoming makes development, [while] yielding leads to decay, the destruction of the organism.

Religiously speaking, all you have to do to go to hell is to do nothing at all. The wind blows that way. Just do as you please, don't resist, gratify all desires, never mind conscience, and hell will be along pretty soon.

Heaven is up hill all the way. But it's keen and bracing exercise. It means a healthier body, livelier mind, and happier spirit every day.

And, at the top of the hill, you get the Morning Star.

It is when we look forward too much and keep expecting results that time alone can give, that we fall into the petulance or fretfulness that destroys the quality of our guidance.
—THE SPIRIT OF THE DAY'S WORK

MORALITY WRONG END TO

Another learned judge has advanced into the newspapers and declares *ex cathedra* that the telephone is corrupting the morals of our youth. Young Bill and Mary can talk much too easily, and the manufacture of "dates" is working overtime. Besides, telephoning greases the wheels of extravagance, since the housewife will not make hash out of the remnants of the roast when she can step to the phone and order a brand-new steak.

This sort of reasoning is not new. There never has been a step made in the improvement of human conditions but some moral monitor arose and pointed out that it would loosen the bonds of virtue.

Cities present greater advantages than the country for business, social life, and amusement; and it is a gray-headed platitude that the city is far more dangerous to young people than the country.

Railways are more convenient than the one-hoss shay; but beware of them! for you might meet someone in the day coach who will speak to you.

Street cars are opportunities for promiscuous acquaintance; better walk; or still better, stay home.

Something ought to be done to protect innocence also from the United States Post office!

The only really moral thing seems to be to lock your child up in the barn and feed him or her through a knot-hole.

This whole system of thought is based upon the erroneous idea that it is a parent's chief duty to keep the child SAFE.

The truth, on the contrary, is that our main task is to train the child for intelligent liberty, to develop his sense of personal responsibility, and to equip him to take care of himself.

The needed lesson in life is to learn how to meet and deal with danger, and not how to avoid danger.

A judicious amount of authority is proper in parents, but if that authority is an end in itself, and if we only seek to teach the child to obey blindly, and do not train his own powers of resistance to evil, we do more harm than good.

Prohibition is right when a child cannot understand; but it is wrong even then when there is no effort to make him understand.

It is not opportunity that threatens the morals of youth; it is ignorance of mind and feebleness of character.

And there is only one way to ensure the moral character and adequate intelligence of the people; and that is to teach ethics in the public schools, to train children there in honesty, cleanliness, and manhood, and to keep all the children during their nonage in school all the time.

Here, as I have pointed out often, is the running sore of our crime, pauperism, and all social evil—namely, our failure to care for the children, and of our thrusting of them, untrained, into the economic struggle.

Go back, teach, train, educate, develop, prevent; and let us have done with this medieval tinkering with telephones, theatres, and picnics to keep people decent!

THE MOSQUITO

Volume 8

Why mosquitoes? We have pondered deeply over the strange things of this existence. We have wondered at cyclones and volcanoes, earthquakes and wars, diseases and poison snakes, but the most amazing phenomenon, in a world supposed to be good in the main, is the mosquito.

Because the poison he injects is for no reason conceivable. It seems to be just pure cussedness.

The rattlesnake strikes to defend himself. The skunk will not distribute his perfumery unless he is in danger. The lion kills for food. Hunger, and not malice, governs the predatory eagle. Even man, the most relentless and successful of brutes, kills cattle for provender and to get leather for his shoes, and shoots grouse ostensibly to adorn his table.

The tornado may be the only way of restoring the equilibrium of the air, and the volcanic eruption may be due to some sort of terrestrial indigestion.

But the mosquito! If it's blood he needs to keep him going we cannot blame him. One way or another all creatures live upon their fellows.

But he doesn't need to poison to get his meal. The poisoning is wholly unnecessary and superfluous.

Besides ungrateful. After filling his maw with my life-fluid he gives me a hypodermic of malaria, as if one would slap my face and say, "Good-by! God bless you!"

Perhaps he doesn't like me. That, too, is his privilege. I don't like him for that matter. But we might well address him in the classic lines:

"Perhaps it was right to dissemble
    your love,
But—why did you kick me down-
    stairs?"

Alas! the moral purpose of the mosquito seems to be to reveal to mankind the fact that the earth is not perfect, nature is not moral, and that heaven is our home.

In other words, we must recognize in life, as in nature, the presence of the purely malicious.

We hate to acknowledge it, it is a bitter pill for the optimist, it is a shattering of our faith in human nature, but it appears to be the unavoidable truth that there are some folks who are just "plain mean."

We see it in children. Even the most angelic of them at times seem to take pleasure in causing pain. Most of them happily get over this. Some don't.

I have known men, I regret to say, who take real pleasure in tormenting their wives.

I have known creatures so full of petty spite they would go out of their way to do someone an evil turn.

There are thugs who beat men for the pleasure of the exercise.

There are teamsters who lash horses until the dumb brutes tremble with agony.

Why dispute as to whether there is a personal devil? Why quarrel about names? There is a somebody or a somewhat that gets into men and women and dehumanizes them, makes them like to hurt people. Call it the devil, call it x—it's there just the same.

So I suppose the mosquito is Nature's antidote for too much optimism.

MULE POWER

Volume 1

There's a deal of talk about will power among uplifters and advisers and exhorters and all the rest of the hecklers of poor, wabbly humanity. There are books on the development of the will, books widely advertised and presumably widely read. Also, books on the diseases of the will.

But there's something much more essential to success here below and salvation up yonder than will power.

It is won't power.

And I'll tell you a secret.

Only the exceptional character has a dominant will. Only a few have will power. But every mother's son of us has won't power aplenty.

Even weaklings. Even we drifty, yielding, oh-be-a-good-fellow, anything-to-be-agreeable, go-with-the-crowd boys and girls—we can be just as strong in our won'ts as the supermen are in their wills.

That's the beauty of it. The good God has so ordered things that the least and peakedest of us can save ourselves as well as the mightiest and greatest. Because all we have to do is DO NOTHING.

To keep out of the horrible pits that beset the human path, all that's necessary is NOT to walk into them.

For instance, the way to quit drinking is simply NOT TO DRINK.

That's all.

Easy!

It does not require struggle and prayer and courage and a grand character and will power. A man can have all these and use them and still coast uninterruptedly down the alcoholic slide.

What it takes to quit, and stay quit, is won't power.

Plain stubbornness.

Mule power.

Behold the mule. As a won'ter he has no equal. Except maybe a woman. Take him for your ideal. Set yourself. Balk!

Say: "They can lead me to the bar, but they can't make me drink. I can suffer. I can crave. I can die. But no power in heaven, on earth, or under the earth can make me swallow the stuff if I simply WON'T."

No matter how vacillating you are, how much of a spineless imbecile and moral wreck you are, there's one thing you can do as powerfully and irresistibly as Julius Cæsar or Napoleon—you can NOT do a thing.

If you'll just see this, and believe it, it may be worth a million dollars to you.

To get out of the spider's web, to get your feet out of the quicksand that's engulfing you, all you have to do is—not anything grand and noble and pious and pure—but just simply use your stubbornness.

USE YOUR MULE POWER.

Glory be to stubbornness!

MUSIC: MAKE IT YOURSELF

Volume 2

The American people are the worst singers in the world, at least as far as my observation goes.

And they are missing a lot of fun. We flatter ourselves that we play more than Europeans. We do not.

For instance, we don't play baseball. We go and see it played. Ditto football and polo.

Our boys and girls play, but once the American passes the hoop and marbles and leap-frog age, he settles down into the capacity of spectator.

He doesn't perform plays; he watches them. He doesn't sing in church, as the English and Germans do; he hires a quartet to sing at him. He doesn't play the fiddle or trombone or clarinet; he goes to listen to hired men who work (not play) on these instruments for a living.

He doesn't take time to learn *Rigoletto* or the *Messiah*, which would provide him not only with immense recreation and most enjoyable refreshment, and also would enable him really to understand the music and unlock for him an infinite treasure of delights; he only goes to hear professionals perform such works.

I doubt if the Metropolitan Opera is of any real cultural value. A lot of experts, mostly foreigners, are hired to sing. We go and listen. Our young people aspire to be like them.

Every big city is full of pitiable boys and girls studying music. I say pitiable, because they aim to make a living by music. Worse, each dreams of distinction, of being a Caruso or a Farrar. Not one in a hundred thousand achieves fame. Not one in ten thousand even becomes able to earn a livelihood.

If, instead of this sad spectacle, we could have great choruses and orchestras where people could sing and play for the joy of it, then music would be a blessing and not a fever.

Why cannot we take up music as a species of fun, to be participated in by ourselves? We don't hire dancers; we do our own foxtrotting. Why can't we make our own music, or at least have our young people learn to do so?

Plato said, "Musical training is a more potent instrument than any other, because rhythm and harmony find their way into the secret places of the soul, on which they mightily fasten."

You do not get the benefits of music unless you make it yourself. To learn to play one of Mendelssohn's *Songs Without Words* will give you more genuine soul-riches than to run off a barrel of records and rolls on the talking-machine and the player-piano.

Whoever will induce our people to sing will do a national service. Oh, the dumb* congregations in church, the dumb audiences in theatres, the dumb soldiers in camps, the dumb crowds in the street! How they would be liberated, fired, invigorated, if they could and would sing!

No force is so great in any man as the stored-up power of what he has been doing every day.
—EVERY DAY

*mute

NATURE'S PURPOSE WITH US IS TO SEE IF WE ARE AFRAID

Volume 2

There is no doubt there is such a thing as a run of luck. To say there is no such thing, and that it only seems so, is to forget the fact that all there is real in the world, to me, is what seems real to me.

Every whist-player knows that he can get hand after hand of low cards during an evening, as though some imp of darkness were shifting all the high cards to his opponents. To try and break the spell he will get up and walk around his chair, or call for a new deck.

There are the proverbs, "It never rains but it pours," and, "Misfortunes never come singly"; and of these we find equivalents in all languages. The thing indicated must be therefore a universal experience.

When we apply our reason to this problem we say at once that it means nothing, that it is mere coincidence, and that the objective phenomenon is probably subjective, a matter of our mood.

And still, in spite of all our reason, we find the belief in it persists; one of those shamefaced half-beliefs, half-superstitions, that lurk in the dark corners of the brain.

I am not going to solve the mystery, because I cannot, which is a most excellent reason. But I wish to suggest one thing.

When luck is running against us, that is the time to play the man. When the unseen powers seem to be handing us clip and tweak and blow, that is the time to pluck up our courage, cinch up our belt, smile, and be unafraid.

For my theory of Nature's purpose is rather fanciful, I fear. It is that she is intent on trying us by every conceivable method, to see if we are afraid. And when a man simply will not get scared, at danger plain or danger spooky, she gives up trying, and hands over to him the keys of the Kingdom.

THE NEED OF CHANGE IN GOVERNMENT

Volume 4

The government ought to be changed. There was never a government that did not need changing. There never will be.

Certain reformers seem to

imagine that if we could get a perfect government the ills of the nation would speedily be cured.

This is merely one form of that enthusiastic but mistaken dream to which in general mankind is prone; to wit, that we ourselves would be ideal if we only had ideal circumstances.

For government is but a circumstance, a part of our environment, one of the outward conditions to which we are subject; a very important one, to be sure.

But we might as well say, if we had an ideal family, or home, or town, or schools, or churches; for all these things mean simply ideal people, which you will probably never find.

We all have the perfect man, the faultless woman in our mind's eye; but we shall never see one with the eye of this flesh. The best we can do is to keep approximating to perfection as best we can.

The ideal government is simply that government where there is the maximum of order with the minimum of constraint.

We approach this only as individuals become by nature more orderly. As the citizen improves in self-control the control of government gradually disappears.

Absolutism and privilege are necessitated by ignorance; only intelligence and altruism can bring about pure democracy.

No Greatness Without Teachableness

Volume 7

About the most hopeful element in any human being's character I should reckon to be teachableness. Whenever you meet a man who knows, and knows he knows, and wards off any proof of reasoning of yours with the impenetrable shield of a superior smile or the dull hostility of a determined eye, you feel that between you and him there can be no real dealings.

A lot of so-called firm faith is merely fixed and rocky egotism. Many a man thinks he has principles when he has nothing but what was a slushy Portland cement of ignorance now hardened into rigid prejudice.

The wisest minds I find are the most teachable. The wider one's experience, the more thorough his study, the braver his heart, and the stronger his intelligence, the more willing he is to hear what you or any man may have to offer.

Stubbornness is usually the instinctive self-defense of conscious weakness. When one can do nothing else to show his strength he imitates the mule, the most despised of animals, sets his feet, lays back his ears, and won't budge.

Of all creatures deliver us from

the man or woman to whom you cannot tell anything!

Spinoza's maxim was that the two great banes of humanity are self-conceit and the laziness coming from self-conceit.

NOTHING'S TOO GOOD TO BE TRUE

Volume 7

Why do you say, "It's too good to be true"?

Don't ever let me hear you say it again, or I will certainly stand you in the corner and make you wear the dunce-cap.

For to make such a remark shows you to be just a plain Gump.

There's nothing too good to be true.

Say that. Repeat it, just as you repeat the Apostles' Creed at church. Keep on saying it morning, noon, and night, until its meaning comes back from the spoken words, and enters the mouth that uttered them, and gets into your system, and purifies your blood, and reorganizes your think-works, and deoppilates* your spleen, and causes you to be born again.

Rid yourself of that subtle superstition that afflicts many an otherwise intelligent person, that silly suspicion that destiny, instead of being your friend, is a huge Dick Deadeye, waiting for you around the next corner with a sandbag.

Fate is your friend. Don't you know that? She is as fond of you as your mother. She is not a sinister, lurking German, waiting to throw a bomb at you.

God is good. The Bible says that the being who is overruling all things is a loving Father. And the Bible stands pretty high among the authorities on God.

Who told you He was an old Ogre? Are you a baby that has been listening to scary stories?

I am here to tell you that this is a wonderful world, full of grand surprises and radiant adventure.

Set your face that way. Look for the happy events.

Somebody is likely to come along and hand you a million dollars, the girl you love will say yes when you ask her, you are going to prosper in business, and you will meet a dark gentlemen (see that Jack of Spades?) who will tell you something to your advantage.

How do I know?

I don't know.

But aren't you a deal happier when you listen to such talk than when you hear said that someone near and dear to you will lose an ear

*unobstructs

next week, or that a trusted friend is going to steal your dress-suit, or that the girl you love will elope with the ice-man?

It's all bunk, you say. Granted, but if you're going a-bunking, for heaven's sake, deal in pleasant bunk.

Where did you get the notion that nothing is truth but tragedy?

As a matter of fact, the most utter frauds going are the calamity-howlers.

Let fate bruise me, and destiny punish me, and the avengers club me; at least they will never have the satisfaction of knowing they frightened me.

Whenever happens I am going to believe that the occult* powers are friendly.

Something good is going to happen tomorrow. Even if it doesn't, the belief in it has helped today.

I say All's well and There's a good time coming, and If I'm a fool I'd rather be a cheerful fool than a fool dismal.

So come along, old man. Cheer up. For there's nothing too good to be true.

ON NEW YEAR'S DAY—TRY AGAIN

Volume 6

The gist of New Year's Day is—Try again.

That's why it rolls around once a year.

That's why we hang a new calendar on the wall, and lay a fresh diary on the desk.

The markings of time have their spiritual significance.

Every clock-tick means that life is not one big rush, one grand gamble, where our all is staked upon some one issue, but it's a step-by-step process, and there are as many opportunities every twenty-four hours as there are seconds; that is to say, that the situation changes daily 86,400 times.

Every clock-stroke says another hour is gone, a new hour is mine, and it may be better than the last. At any rate, whatever we have to do, it's only one hour at a time.

Life as a lump is too much for any of us. It is a burden to break any man's back. But one hour—we can stand that—and that is all we have to stand. So come on, boys, we'll go through one hour of it, and we will not tackle the second hour until it comes to meet us.

Every day is a new life. Every evening is a day of judgment. Every morning is a resurrection. One day is all there is to it, and that isn't so much.

*imperceptible

We don't have to eat a whole beef—just a slice. Nor to drink up the river—just a glassful. Nor to jump a mile—just a step at a time.

And all these minor markings are lumped and emphasized by New Year's Day.

The past year is gone. It's dead. We are living. The past is God's. The future is ours.

All our mistakes, humiliations, failures, follies, and stupidities; our jealousies and heart-breaks, our wounds and bruises; all the whole league of miseries that make life lame and weary; all, all are gone, swallowed up in that big, black hole we call the past, submerged in the same dark waters where lie Cæsar and his legions, Abelard and Heloise, Solomon, and Tubal Cain.

On New Year's Day let us put on our "morning faces." Let us begin again with all things new—babies and chicks, furry kittens and cubs, youth and adventure!

The sun is climbing. The wind's right from heaven. Love is newborn daily while hate grows old.

Come, kiss and make up! Drop the past, as your night garment, and put on the fresh clothing of hope. Wash your face in the cool waters of faith—it's ever running, runs out from under the Great White Throne, and runs through the city streets.

Come! No more tears and regrets. Take your hat, old friend, and come with me. We'll go and meet the adventurous future.

Undismayed and unafraid we'll greet the New Year.

THE PART OF ME THAT DOUBTS

Volume 7

Whatever a man's creed, there's a good deal of him that does not believe it. Whatever a man's crime, there was some of him that protested. Whatever a man's goodness, it is flecked on the underside with ugly spots. Let us deal reverently with one another, and with awe; we are all so complex. It should not be so hard to believe in God, for man himself is scarcely

less wonderful.

The universe is just as great and amazing inside of me as outside. Immanuel Kant marveled when he looked into his own heart, as when he looked up at the sky. So the stars over me are no less sublime than my soul which mirrors them; thunder and lightning among the clouds are matched by storms of passion within me as terrible as they; my memory is a greater thing than the British Museum, for it is a living museum; my will is greater than gravitation or electricity or gunpowder, for it can use them, and they cannot budge it; my imagination is more wondrous than the Vatican gallery, for its pictures come and go with instant swiftness, and my conscience is as mysterious and as majestic as the substance of God Himself.

Let a man reverence himself. Then he is not far from believing in God.

THE PAST

Volume 9

A good deal of morbid nonsense has been said and written and thought about the past.

The past is irrevocable, we have been told in sermon and story—you cannot escape the past—the past can never be changed—and so on, and so on—the whole trend of this thought being that the past is a kind of Sherlock Holmes dogging our steps forever, a sinister nemesis waiting its chance to strike us down, the account-book of an angry God sure to confront us some day.

All of this is morbid, most of it is dramatic; the underlying sentiment of it is false, weakening, and septic.

As a matter of fact, our past, as Maeterlinck says, depends upon our present and changes with it.

What the past is depends upon the way you are now using it. Its effect upon your destiny will be gauged by how you translate it into the future.

If we brood over the past, and weaken ourselves with vain regrets, with self-contempt and remorse, then it will poison and undo us.

But no matter what it contains of our sin or folly, we can, by a right use of it now, make it minister to our welfare.

First, we can learn wisdom from it. By it we can realize our faults to be corrected and our offenses to be atoned for. And with this wisdom we can go on [to] better things.

The only true repentance is so to use the past as to enable us to build a better future. Weeping and wailing and brooding are the luxuries of morbidity.

The past is beneath our feet. We can go down into it and wallow in impotent grief, or we can step upon it to higher things.

The great enemy of life is despair. The great friend of life is hope. Despair paralyzes, ruins. Hope energizes, "for we are saved by hope."

Up! Face the future! Whatever the past has been, let it nerve you to spend your remaining days in faithfulness and loyalty to your better self!

So Tennyson, with clear insight, with sane instinct for moral truth, wrote:

"I hold it truth, with him (Goethe)
    who sings
To one clear harp in divers tones,
That men may rise on stepping-
    stones
Of their dead selves to higher
    things."

PAY, PAY, PAY!

Volume 7

Whatever you get you pay for, one way or another.

The cheapest plan is to pay cash.

There is a sort of satisfaction in giving money down for anything. Then you feel the matter is settled. No mortgage on your future happiness "heavy, heavy, hangs over your head."

Think over all the things you ever got for nothing. You've paid for them every one; paid perhaps in lowered self-respect, restricted liberty, an embarrassing sense of obligation—something that has cost you more than if you had handed over the price at once.

Stolen waters are sweet. The trouble is, nobody ever got away with them. Every ounce of sweetness made a pound of nausea.

Self-indulgence tastes good. But remember the price: self-loathing.

Pride is a comfortable sensation. But its price is a fall, which is not comfortable.

When you do what you know is shady, in order to gain money or other advantage, you get your desire maybe, but it is prostitute's pay. You've sold yourself, and that is always a fool's bargain.

Nature keeps books pitilessly. Your credit with her is good, but she collects; there is no land you can flee to and escape her bailiffs.

You can cheat Nature, abuse her, lie to her, overreach her—she is very complaisant; you may do your will with her, but she never forgets; she sees to it that you pay her every cent you owe, with interest.

Every day her bloodhounds track down the men and women who owe her. The newspapers are full of their shrieks of pain, their gestures of horror.

Every generation a new crop of fools comes on. They think they can beat the orderly universe. They conceive themselves to be more clever than the eternal laws. They snatch goods from Nature's store and run. They enjoy the booty, laugh and cackle at their skill.

And one by one they all come back to Nature's counter and pay—pay in tears, in agony, in despair; pay as fools before them have paid.

There is a perpetual, persistent ignorance, as eternal as wisdom.

So, enjoy yourself, youth; eat, drink, and be merry, and let your soul delight itself in fatness and wine, pluck the bloom of beauty, and gather the fruits of laughter; but count the cost, beware of the insidious credit system, and pay cash.

At least then you'll know what it costs.

PEACE WITHIN

Volume 6

You are tired of the turmoil? You want to escape the din and strife? You long for peace?

Then learn that the only peace that is full of rest, that means poise and calm energy, is inward peace.

The real peace may be found in the marketplace, the hustings, the battlefield. There men strive and cry. There are smoke and dust, the hurrying messenger, the panting wrestler. But in the heart of the man who has found himself is the spot of calm.

On the contrary, one may be in a remote wilderness, "far from the madding crowd's ignoble strife," alone with the twilight and the vast silences of nature, and yet be torn by the winds of passion or shaken by the thunders of fear.

A wise man will not seek peace without, but peace within. He will still the turbulence of desire, hold in leash the dogs of impatience, drive off the harpies of egotism, screen his soul from the mosquitoes of irritation, scotch the snakes of revenge, destroy the scorpions of self-pity, and with the copious draughts of courage and pure faith ward off the fevers of fear, the chills of cowardice, the manias of superstition.

Peace! Peace within! The mother has it, serene among her fretful children. The merchant has it; amidst the clatter of affairs, the lust of gain, and the hurt of loss, his heart is an unruffled pool; so is he always ready, at his best, unrouted, though about him are the stampede and panic.

The boy has it; the fires flame, the pack is in full cry, the horn is sounding, but he stands, smiling and firm as a mountain peak in the morning, for his heart is fixed, and the swirl of folly cannot move his feet.

The little school-teacher has it, and at the end of the day, when the others come fagged and frayed from the clamor of obstreperous young life, she appears in the sweetness of victory, unshattered, with her untouched soul clean and strong.

The soldier has it; shells burst about him, death hisses in the speeding bullet, corpses fester, war's discomfort pulls at him, and war's fury pounds him, but his eye is clear, his lips are smiling and unafraid, his hand is steady, his brain precise, for his heart is hid with a great thought, wrapped in the folds of a beautiful ideal.

Peace! Peace within! Give me that, and let accusing tongues wag and envious hands tear, let the storms blow and the floods mount, and I shall be happy as a child in its mother's arms.

What deep wisdom and riches in the last words of the departing Teacher when He said: "Peace I leave with you, my peace I give unto you: not as the world giveth, give I unto you. Let not your heart be troubled, neither let it be afraid."

PLEASURE AND CONTENTMENT

Volume 5

A good deal of the discontent of all of us is of a piece with that of the little girl who wanted it to be Christmas every day.

We over-emphasize the value of climaxes and under-estimate the value of contentment.

Souls that are often white-hot burn out. It is better to be always a little warm.

The women who shed the most joy in the world of men, by the spending of their treasure, are not they who stir volcanic passions, but they who are creatures

"Not too bright nor good
For human nature's daily food."

The drinkables that conduce most to human well-being are those that make you comfortable, and not those that make you drunk.

The religious feeling which is most useful is not the kind that wades through dark valleys of doubt and violence, but the kind that sheds the daily warm sunshine of faith and cheer over all the common days.

A man has learned much when he has left off seeking pleasure and begun seeking contentment.

POISONING THE CHILD MIND

One of the recent discoveries in the art of healing is the therapeutic value of suggestion. That is to say, the physician, by suggesting to the patient, particularly the patient suffering from nervous disorder, sane and helpful thoughts about himself, can work a cure better oftentimes than by the use of drugs.

The force of mental suggestion is so great that many fads, and even new religions, have arisen which are based upon it.

If the influence of good suggestion be so great, the influence of bad suggestion is even greater.

I wish to call attention to one form of character poisoning of which parents are frequently guilty.

Perhaps the worst misfortune that can happen [to] a person is to be infested with germs of fear, to lack decision and self-confidence, to be a prey to the terrors of morbidity and doubt of self. Who can tell the mortal pain, shame, and self-torture of the innumerable victims of chronic fear?

Frequently parents are responsible for this. A boy, for instance, develops some inborn trait of waywardness; he is untruthful, will not apply himself, is careless, disobedient, or persists in keeping bad company; the parent naturally tells him of his fault, and, as it seems to do no good, drops into a constant practise of scolding. Over and over the boy is reminded that he is "bad," that he will never amount to anything, and so on. This finally filters in the child's subconsciousness, and then the irretrievable damage; for when he comes to believe in his sub-mind that he is bad, he is bad.

Why not try to find the CAUSE of your child's defects and remove it? When you KNOW that blame and reproof do no good, why go on?

We do not realize that it is a CRIME to say to any child, under any circumstances, that he is bad, weak, or vicious. When you do that you are planting a seed of damage in his mind.

Many a woman has been wrecked because her life was poisoned when she was a child by unceasing mental suggestions from her mother that she was naughty, wicked, unreliable, or untruthful.

Many a man is a weak failure in the struggles of mature life simply because the cult of failure was carefully instilled into his childish mind by his thoughtless parents.

Dwell upon and encourage the good that is in your child. Ignore his defects as far as possible. Learn how to shut your eyes. Above all, do not tell him he is wicked. Show him his faults, but never in public, but in sacred intimacy. Show him the consequences of wrongdoing; but enlist his aid in opposing his bad traits. Persistently suggest to him that he is good, brave, strong, and truthful. In after-life this belief of yours in him will tone up his self-respect and give him strength in his hours of crisis.

POVERTY

Volume 9

The other day I met one of those all too common persons, a poor rich man. He owned several farms, besides houses in town, stocks and bonds in the vault, and money in the bank.

Yet he was poor. He had the essence of poverty in his mind. Because he was afraid he might come to want, because he was suspicious of everybody, because he worried over his possessions, and because he wanted more.

For poverty is not lack of things; it's a state of mind.

Rich folks are not they who have abundance, but they who feel abundance. As a man thinketh, so is he.

You are rich only when money doesn't worry you. And if you have only two dollars, and don't fret over what you do not have, you are richer than the man who has two million dollars and can't sleep o' nights because he hasn't four million dollars.

Poverty is not lack; it is the pressure of lack.

Poverty is in the mind; not in the pocket.

This poor rich man I spoke of was fretting over the grocer bills, and the cost of ice and gas and electricity. He was fighting to keep down the wages of the servants. It hurt him when his wife wanted money. He complained because his daughters spent so much. The demands of his workmen for more wages pained him like a sore toe. He haggled over the price of everything he bought.

In fine, he had every last one of the symptoms and inconveniences of poverty that his washerwoman had. And more. And if he felt the pangs of poverty, and if money worried him, and made him miserable, can you tell me what difference there is between him and a hobo?

The only use of money is to give you ease and comfort, to drive away your fears, and enable you to live in spiritual freedom. If it does not that, then, no matter how rich they may call you, you are poor.

And, if you can have that feeling of freedom, that sure belief in tomorrow, that sense of abundance, which money is supposed to bring, but hardly ever does bring, and if you can have all this just by using your will power, and changing your attitude of mind, in other words, by rich thinking, which is easily attained, instead of by accumulation, which is slow and laborious and uncertain, isn't this "the more excellent way"?

Think on this! If you want to be rich, why, BE RICH; it's easier than GETTING RICH. Try it.

THE POWER OF RIGHT IDEAS

Volume 1

It does make a difference what you think. Sometimes you hear it said that it does not and that all that matters is what you do; that your opinions are nobody's business.

Your ideas are of the utmost importance. What's in your mind directly affects the work of your hands. What you believe alters what you see and hear.

In fact, every sensation, every fact coming into your brain mixes with the contents already there and forms a sort of chemical compound with the notions on hand; and it is this compound, this combination of actual fact and previous conviction, which finally gets into your ego and forms your conclusion.

So your duty is not first to get the facts and to see the truth. Your first duty is to prepare yourself to do this. If your mind is full of false ideas, if it is clouded with superstition or twisted by false sentiment, or all hard and brittle because of some non-fact to which you have given your "faith" from a sense of duty, you are entirely incapable of using the truth.

Clean up inside.

How?

Well, be intellectually honest for one thing. There's an ethics of the intellect as well as of the heart. Don't lie to yourself, or cozen yourself, or hypnotize yourself. Once you accept a thing as true, without knowing whether it is true or not, you are on the road to mental ruin.

As Clifford says, "Belief is desecrated when given to unproved and unquestioned statements for the solace and private pleasure of the believer."

Second, test every new fact by comparing it with other facts that you have tried out and are sure of. The new one ought to fit. If it does not you may well suspect there is something wrong. It is the essence of sanity to look around and see how a supposed fact gets along with its relatives. It is the essence of insanity to hang on to one idea without reference to others.

Third, believe in the truth, that it is always safer than expediency, and that it is vastly more important that a thing be true than that it be profitable or pleasant or even practicable.

The truth shall make you free.

An untruth always tangles you up.

Truth is the logic of the universe; it is the reasoning of destiny; it is the mind of God. And nothing that you can devise or discover can take its place.

Get right ideas.

If you don't, you're all wrong.

PRAGMATISM

Volume 3

Action is the father of thought. We do not learn all about a thing and then go and do it; we do it first, badly perhaps, and keep on doing it; and out of the doing of a thing comes the understanding of it.

Truth is not found by study, nor by searching for it, least of all by the idle and "do-less"; it is a sort of liquor that is secreted by the concrete deed.

Hence students, investigators, and theorists are proverbially cautious. With them everything depends. It is said of James Buchanan that he was so circumspect that if you asked him whether the sun had arisen that morning, he would answer, "Well, that, of course, depends upon where one is standing on the earth."

Now, there is none of this hesitancy about a blacksmith. He knows what he can do with red-hot iron, because he has tried it. His knowledge came not by memorizing or speculating, it is the product of sweat, fire, and hammer. The real "learned class" consists of farmers, butchers, bakers, and candlestick-makers. What they know they know. The so-called "learned professions" are composed of doctors and lawyers and preachers, who are all more or less expert guessers.

This is the gist of what is called pragmatism, which means, in plain English, that truth is not a thing, like a pebble or a fish, to be picked up or caught. Hence you can never squeeze it into a statement. Truth is a relation, like a sine or a cosine; it is a sort of color or perfume attached to and growing out of a deed. Hence truth is what will work; error is what will not work. The only way to tell one from the other is to try them and see. Sometimes it takes a thousand years, and battles, and epochs of madness, and kingdoms and republics, and a whole world to try them out.

PRAISE

Praise is never wholly undeserved.

Don't be afraid. No bonds were ever broken by appreciative remarks.

Go ahead. Say it. You can hardly come in contact with anybody without noting some commendable thing. Speak of it.

And if any criticism, any salt or sour word comes up in your throat, swallow it back.

What a vast, kindly, benevolent, bottomless pit is the pit of the great unsaid! It is the Gehenna valley of our lives, where lie the burnt refuse of our unkindness. You are full of gentle thoughts and gentle words, only you do not realize how full until you begin to speak.

Unstop your generous impulses. Turn on the fountain of your praise.

For this world of human hearts is dry and dusty. Most men and women go about smitten with a cruel thirst. The sons and daughters of men perish for appreciation.

Then water them. Sprinkle them with the gentle rain of your cheering words. Drop the dew of your admiring glances and warm smiles on the just and upon the unjust, with heaven's indiscrimination.

Contrtwist you, smile!

We Americans are an odd lot. We are soft as wax in our hearts, full of generous feeling, hungry to help the next man. But we hate to admit it.

I have walked the city street, in lonely moods, and searched the face of every passerby for a human look. But it was dreary picking. Men glanced at me and looked quickly away. Women never looked at all. Only a woman or two of Mrs. Warren's profession. And I have wondered if it is not sheer loneliness, mere desire to see a lighted face, even if it must be bought, and not a taste for vice, that leads men to take up with crepuscular creatures.

For souls are purchased with kindness. Every cordial gesture you make to a man gives you a property-right to a portion of his soul.

Mine are the people I have loved, if only for a moment. They constitute my estate. I own them. I do not own my purse.

" 'Twas mine, 'tis his, and has been slave to thousands." I do not own my house, the contents of my strong box, my furniture and pictures, no, nor the wife I have legally bound to me, nor the children I have begotten, save in so far as I love them.

There is but one right and title in the court of souls. It is love. It is appreciation. Anything or anybody in this world belongs to the one who appreciates it, or him, or her. No other claim will stand in the great assizes.

And I do not own those who appreciate me; they own me. It is the lover, and not the beloved, that has the best end of the bargain. Love is its own reward.

Hence, get rich. Pile up property.

Be a soul millionaire. Do this by the practise of appreciation. Be an appreciation expert. The wider, more refined, subtler, keener your power to see the praiseworthiness of men and things, the wealthier you are. Be a Hetty Green in appreciation.

Compliment. Appreciate. Praise. But me no buts. No praise is ever wholly undeserved.

A PRAYER FOR VISION

Volume 9

O Lord, open thou mine eyes. Cure my blindness, that I may see past the tall buildings of cities and perceive the souls thereof, past the dark material into the luminous spiritual, past the hard things visible unto the fluid, eternal things invisible.

All about me are the barriers that cut off men's view of the wide vistas. Make mine eyes to have X-ray power to pierce through, and to be like telescopes to see afar.

Let me see beyond the quick satisfaction of hate to the long joy of forgiveness. Let me see beyond appetite to the pleasure of self-control. Let me see beyond greed to the luxury of giving. Past gold to the treasures of contentment.

Widen my horizon. Give me largeness of heart.

Let me not love the one woman less, but through her the welfare of all women.

All around and about my own children stand innumerable children everywhere; may my vision reach them, that I may strive to live for them also.

Let me see past revenge unto the strength and wisdom of forgiveness.

Let me see past blinding pride to sunny healthfulness of humility.

Let me see past profit to usefulness.

Past success to self-approval;

Past passion to poise;

Past the heat of desire to the light of renunciation;

Past the glare of power to the abiding beauty of service;

Past the rank, poisonous growth

of self to the fragrance and flowers of unself.

Take my life out of the narrow pit and set me upon a high mountain.

I want to see, to see, and not forever to be a prisoner of prejudice, a bat of blind custom, a mote of ignorance, a convict in the penitentiary of fear, a frightened rat in the house of superstition.

Let me see beyond the boundaries of my country unto all the world;

Past competition to cooperation, past war to world government;

Past party to patriotism;

Past patriotism to humanity.

Let me see past the night to the renewing dawn;

Past gloom to glory, past death to eternal life, past the finite to the infinite;

Past men and things and events to God.

PRECEDENT

Precedent is solidified experience. In the realm of ideas it is canned goods.

It is very useful when fresh ideas are not to be had.

There are advantages in doing things just because they always have been done. You know what will happen. When you do new things you do not know what will happen.

Success implies not only sound reasoning, but also the variable factor of how a thing will work, which is found out only by trying it.

Hence, the surest road to success is to use a mixture of precedent and initiative. Just how much of each you will require is a matter for your judgment.

To go entirely by precedent you become a mossback. You are safe, as a setting hen or a hiving bee is safe. Each succeeding generation acts the same way. There is a level of efficiency, but no progress.

Boards, trustees, and institutions lay great stress upon precedent, as they fear responsibility. To do as our predecessors did shifts the burden of blame a bit from our shoulders.

The precedent is the haven of refuge for them that fear to decide.

Courts of law follow precedent, on the general theory that experience is more just than individual decision.

Precedent, however, tends to carry forward the ignorance and injustice of the past.

Mankind is constantly learning, getting new views of truth, seeing new values in social justice. Precedent clogs this advance. It fixes and perpetuates the wrongs of man as much as the rights of man.

Hence, while the many must trust to precedent, a few must always endeavor to break it, to make way for juster conclusions.

Precedent is the root, independent thinking is the branch of the human tree. Our decisions must conform to the sum of human experience, yet there must be also the fresh green leaf of present intelligence.

We cannot cut the root of the tree and expect it to live, neither can we lop off all the leafage of the tree and expect it to live.

The great jurist, such as Marshall, is one who not only knows what the law is, but what the law ought to be. That is, to his knowledge of precedent he adds his vision of right under present conditions.

Precedent is often the inertia of monstrous iniquity. War, for instance, is due to the evil custom of nations who go on in the habit of war-preparedness. The problem of the twentieth century is to batter down this precedent by the blows of reason, to overturn it by an upheaval of humanity.

Evil precedent also lurks in social conditions, in business, and in all relations of human rights. The past constantly operates to enslave the present.

We must correct the errors of our fathers if we would enable our children to correct ours.

Our reverence for the past must be continually qualified by our reverence for the future.

We are on our way to the Golden Age. The momentum of what has been must be supplemented by the steam of original conviction, and guided by the intelligence and courage of the present.

THE PRICE OF LIBERTY

Volume 3

The price of liberty, as quoted, is eternal vigilance. It is more; it is universal vigilance. Nobody can be free unless everybody is free.

Which point I wish to sharpen and hammer in.

The trouble with most people's notion about liberty is that it is too individual.

When a person does as he pleases, has no law but his own will, there results such a clash and confusion that in the end the only one who gets any liberty is the strongest. In carrying out his will he reduces the others to slavery.

The only possible way for the many to get liberty is for them to unite so as to compel the substitution of justice and the general good for the will of the strongest.

This explains why the whole world became involved in a war with Germany. It was because German liberty means liberty for nobody else—Belgium, for instance.

It is also the reason why the United States went into the war. Some simpleminded ones ask why we over here could not go along minding our own business and keep out of the European imbroglio. The answer is that there would not be liberty in this country very long if there were liberty nowhere else in the world.

German policy had already begun to cause the sinking of our unarmed ships upon the high seas.

It also explains conscription, why Congress was justified in requiring every male between the ages of twenty-one and thirty-one to take up arms.

At first blush this seemed a wanton, arbitrary interference with individual rights, compelling by force even ultra-pacifists and German sympathizers and anarchists to be soldiers when they though soldiering in this instance or soldiering

in general to be wrong. But a little reflection will convince one that if there's to be freedom for all everyone must cooperate to secure it.

This also shows why democracy can be successful only when every individual in it discharges his public duties.

Any group of non-voting persons in a democracy is a menace.

All women should have full civic rights, because women being disfranchised accept the protection yet avoid the responsibilities of government. Women should vote, not because some want to, but because all ought to.

Slavery is a danger to any nation, because it makes a politically non-active group of inhabitants.

Any group or class, for whatever reason, that does not participate in public responsibilities is dangerous—including slaves, women, the idle rich, the highbrows who despise politics, and the anarchists who don't believe in government.

And the same principle holds true of the world. The world will never be "safe for democracy" until the last autocratic government is removed.

Liberty is a boat we're all in. A leak anywhere will sink it.

Pride is the stupidest of human perversions.

—PRIDE

PRIDE

Volume 8

Pride is the stupidest of human perversions.

Self-esteem is essential; but in the wise man it is made beautiful by a sincere humanity, while in the fool it is hardened and uglified by ignorance.

Pride has as many forms as the devil. In each it apes some virtue—as does the devil also.

Much that we call patriotism is a diseased national egotism. It is not patriotism that leads men to shoot those of another country; it is vicious self-conceit.

Whoever despises another is an egotist. If we seek to understand those we meet, instead of seeking to dominate, regulate, or judge them, we shall love everybody, even criminals.

The first business of a judge, a preacher, a teacher, or a parent is to understand. This cannot be done without humility.

The prime trait of a gentleman is that he does not have a keen sense of his deserts. The man who thinks he deserves the devotion of a good woman, the adoration of children, and the loyalty of friends, ought to be kicked, as R. L. Stevenson said. A real man is surprised constantly and grateful for all proofs of love.

The fanatic is a person wholly drunk with pride of opinion. It is wrong to call him a man of faith, for no one can have faith who is not willing to hear the other side.

The cheapest form of virtue is that which loves to talk of itself. It is also suspicious.

One who is always prating of purity may well be suspected of inwardly leaning a bit toward uncleanness. The bully is a coward at heart.

It is hard to be envied and criticized, but it is worse to be universally praised. Few men can stand praise without becoming vain and self-centered.

A real man gives himself out to be just what he is. A proud man is a liar, for he wants to be esteemed for more than he is.

Pride is the one thing, more than all others, that offends people. Nobody sympathizes with a proud man. Everybody instinctively wants to take him down a peg. He is ridiculous. Everybody laughs when he stubs his toe.

Pessimism is a form of pride. It is usually held by persons of disordered lives. Pessimism is the religion of the underworld. It is always, in whoever manifests it, a symptom of spiritual dirt.

The proverb says that pride goeth before a fall. That is because pride is stupid; it is an offensive form of mania; the man who has it is approaching a downfall.

When we become conscious of a fault and are filled with humility, that fault is not noticeable to others; but faults leap in the eyes of our friends when our own pride refuses to see them.

Humble, inconspicuous people, those who are in no way celebrities, are usually much pleasanter companions than the famous, because they take criticism kindly and strive to amend.

The notion that assurance and push and forwardness get most out of life is erroneous. Nothing accomplishes more in the long run than genuine modesty.

PRINCIPLES

Principles are the deep laws underlying life.

Just as gravitation runs through every particle of matter from sun to sand grain, just as electricity pervades all things, and chemical affinity works always and everywhere, so there are certain laws that eternally operate in events and in men's minds.

That honesty is the best policy, that courage is power, that practise brings efficiency, and that truth eventually prevails over error, are just as evergreen and exceptionless as the forces in dead stones and planets.

The first business of one who would succeed is to find out these principles, his second business is to believe in them, and his final business is to entrust his whole career to them.

A fool believes in a principle when he sees that it works for his good. A man of sense believes in a principle when he cannot see. The very essence of faith-power is that is works in the dark.

The real man believes most of all in honesty when it is plain that to lie would profit him; believes most of all in cleanliness when the allurements of uncleanliness make their strongest appeal; believes most of all in the power of good to overcome evil when men most clamor for the false remedy of cruel retaliation.

The man of principle steers his course by the north star; in storm and fog he goes straight on; he is an ocean-goer. The man of shrewdness and expediency* is a coaster and explores the deeps at his peril.

One gets the good out of a principle only when he is convinced that

*moral weakness; cares only for himself

it is invariable. Behind it is the eternal will of the universe, which cannot be fooled, tricked, nor dodged.

Rooted in principles life grows stronger and more majestic every day; the years harden it; failures fructify it; the windy blasts toughen it; Junes fill it with flowers, and Octobers load it with fruit.

Take stock of yourself. Are there some big things you utterly believe in, and by them govern your days? Out of those things shall grow your happiness and your usefulness at the last.

Do you think everything has exceptions? Are you straight or crooked as occasion dictates? Do you say, "It all depends"? Are you an opportunist? Do you simply act as your judgment decides in each case? Do you think the end justifies the means; that is, that your little mind is clearer than the omniscient mind?

Do you do that which is EXPEDIENT, or that which is RIGHT?

If you have no principles you are but the chaff which the wind driveth away.

THE PROCESSION OF SOULS

Volume 1

Before us passes the procession of acquaintances. Souls rise and set in our ken like stars. Life is a string of beads, each bead a human spirit whom we come, more or less, to know. They range through all degrees of intimacy, some very close, as husband and wife and children, who are like sun and moon; and friends, our kind of folks, who are like planets, members of our solar system; and acquaintances, some clear as fixed stars, some dim as stars of the fifth magnitude; and back of all these the infinite, numberless galaxies of people, whom we call the nation, the world. In this universe of souls our souls swim.

Life is a wheel, a moving panorama. Every day out of the welter of indiscriminate multitudes there comes to you a new face, perhaps a new customer at your store, a chance acquaintance on the train, someone you fall in with in the hotel lobby or on a steamship, a tramp at your back door, a new girl at your school, someone to whom you are introduced at a friend's house, and so on. All together their number is not great. I wonder if it is written just which souls, of all the millions, shall touch ours. And each one whose personality impinges upon ours, even in the least, leaves some particles of flavor of himself upon us, and we upon him.

The Quitters

History is full of quitters. They furnish some of the most spectacular characters upon the world stage.

It is an illustrious roll-call: Elijah, Jonah, Pilate, Romola, Charles V., Hamlet—and how about you?

Some of these quit only temporarily and took hold again. With the others the quitting was fatal.

Running away and giving up were never a noble business.

The side-stepper does not cut an edifying figure.

At one time men imagined the ills of the world might be cured by deserting the world. They retired into caves and walled retreats. They gave mankind up as a hopeless lot and devoted themselves to getting themselves plucked as brands from the burning.

In Bunyan's *Pilgrim's Progress,* Christian is pictured fleeing his city and family, his fingers in his ears, bound for heaven.

The world has got over this unwisdom. The church now sends missionaries into the world. Social reformers go and live in the slums. These systems indicate a healthier idea.

The question whether the world's progress will be furthered best by our activity or by our desertion need not be discussed. Humanity will doubtless continue to advance whether you and I assist or not. Destiny has its own long plans; and if one man will not play the part it assigns him, another will be found who will do quite as well.

The only question is, not what will happen to the universe, but what will happen to me if I refuse to work. As Mordecai said to Esther when she hesitated to intercede with the king for her people, so it might be said to you or me: "If thou altogether holdest thy peace at this time, doubtless deliverance shall arise from another place, but thou and thy father's house shall be destroyed."

The point is that one's fullest enjoyment of life is only found in fighting courageously in that small corner of the battlefield where he has been stationed. No man ever found worthy content by running away.

To quit implies moral weakness.

Sensitiveness is not to be coddled, but to be overcome.

Go on, forget your wounds, never mind the bruises upon your soul, despise the danger, drop regret, brush aside premonitions, do your work, and you will get a quality of joy the deserter cannot know.

They say the sharks will shy off from a man if he keeps splashing about lively. The fear-birds will not settle upon a soul in vigorous movement.

The noblest drop of consolation that can cheer one's last hour is to say, whether he has won or lost, "I have fought the good fight."

THE REAL AMERICAN

Volume 2

What is a real American? He is a patriot, not a partisan.

He votes.

He pays his taxes honestly.

He keeps informed on public questions.

He is clean of race prejudice, and wants the black man or the yellow man to have equal privilege and opportunity with himself.

He hates militarism, but is ready to serve in army or navy when his country is at war.

His heart beats a little faster when he sees the stars and stripes.

He is made up of three spiritual ingredients: Washington, Franklin, Lincoln.

He respects women, any woman.

He looks you straight in the eye, and says plainly what he thinks.

He honors those who work, and has a wholesome contempt for idlers.

He speaks slowly, and means a little more than he says.

He is tolerant of anything except intolerance.

He does not care what your religious belief is, so long as you are decent.

He has a humor of his own, but laughs with his eyes more than with his mouth.

He is a good loser.

Once in four years he goes on a political debauch, yielding himself up to the most primitive and narrow party spirit; but when it is over he is once more an American, forgets his late passions, and is for the man who was elected, no matter which party was successful.

He is an essential democrat; that is, his creed is not "I am as good as anybody," but is "Anybody is as good as I."

He likes to make money, but likes to see everybody around him making money also. He does not enjoy riches in the midst of poverty.

He wants a family of his own, a business of his own, a house of his own, and an opinion of his own.

His is not a stock, or a race, or a breed; it is a spirit. His parents may be French, Italian, Czech, Polish, or German; but he has caught another spirit: he has been born again; he is an American.

He is a reformer, not a revolutionist.

He hates class.

When laws do not suit him he does not break them; he changes them.

His is the newest nation; his is the youth of humanity.

He is loyal—to his family, to his friend, and to his country.

But his loyalty does not imply lying and spying, cruelty and inhumanity.

He wants nothing for his own country he would not be willing for other countries to have for themselves.

He does not want the United States to rule the world, but to be the big brother to the world.

THE REAL ARISTOCRAT

The idea of an aristocracy, or a superior class, has always been in the world's mind. Nobles, or high-born ones, or some sort of upper four hundred—every nation in history has had them.

The Jews had their Levites, the Japanese their Samurai, the Romans their Patricians. The caste system in one form or another exists today in every European country. Even our USA democracy has its plutocrats, every city its smart set, and every hamlet its upper-crusters.

When there is so much smoke there must be some fire. There is a superior order of beings. The trouble is that those we call superior are—only so called; they are really common as mud, most of them.

For it is not money that makes one really superior, nor birth, nor culture, nor genius, nor intellect, nor place—one may be quite vulgar and have any of these advantages.

To know the real aristocrat, watch for these ten marks:

1. SIMPLICITY. The aristocratic soul loves simple pleasures, not because he cannot have the complex ones, but because greatness naturally chooses simplicity. These things indicate a vulgar nature, to wit: Expensive, highly seasoned, and elaborate foods; costly or showy clothes; the wearing or owning of much jewelry; fondness of perfumes; a taste for luxury and display. The curse of great wealth is not that it is a sin, but that it usually vulgarizes one's nature.

2. SERVICE. The inborn leaning of a high soul is toward serving; of a cheap soul toward being served.

The moral strength of the race is in them that work; the ills of humanity flow from its idle class. If there were no idlers there would be no war, no poverty, and no privilege.

3. CHARACTER. A great soul exercises his influence over his fellows by what he is, not by what he has, nor by the position he holds.

4. The true aristocrat is ABOVE HIS PLEASURES. He enjoys things, but he can quit any minute. The hosts of the petty-souled are driven by their desires.

5. The great soul has NO BITTERNESS. Pessimism is a fever of the small-minded. It is due not only to lack of vision, but to an inherent inability to appreciate the dominant force of goodness. Self-pity, self-depreciation, despair—these, too, are traits of commonness. The genuinely high-born nature cannot slump into them.

6. The true aristocrat can be told by the way he acts toward his superiors and inferiors. In the organization of society everyone finds some above him in station and some below. The elect soul knows how to conduct himself toward his superiors so as to preserve his own self-respect, and toward his inferiors so as not to break down theirs.

7. The gentleman is CLEAN-MINDED. Dirt does not stick to him. His soul cleanses itself like a cat. So it was said of Lincoln, "His heart was as broad as the world, yet it had no room in it for the memory of a wrong." The great-souled cannot retain a grudge, nor remember a slander, nor take a vicious or unclean hint.*

8. TRUTH. The real great ones never want to be appreciated at more than they are worth. They do not show off. They want to be known for exactly their actual value—or less. The little ones want to "make a good showing."

9. The high-minded do not MEDDLE. They do not want to know other people's concerns. They are reluctant to improve, reform, or regulate their neighbors. But they are courteous, thoughtful, and ready with help when help is sought.

10. Finally, the exceptional folk are they with whom FAMILARITY DOES NOT BREED CONTEMPT. The better you know them the more you value them.

How many such spiritual aristocrats do you know? How many of these marks do you find in yourself?

The fact is that happiness does not come from the big events of life, but is made up of innumerable little things.

—HIDDEN HAPPINESS

*suggestion; opportunity

A Real Man

You may never get to be president of the United States, son; you may never be the head of a big business and sit at a mahogany desk and clip coupons; you may never be a hero in war or a fad in literature; but you can be greater than any of these—you can be a Real Man.

And the beauty of it is that, in regard to this one most important attainment in the world, you actually have the whole matter in your own hands. You can be a Real Man if you wish. Nobody can stop you. Heredity cannot trip you. And the circumstances in which you are placed make not the slightest difference.

As for being elected governor, maybe you can make it, maybe not. As for succeeding in business, that is never an absolute surety. Perhaps you can be healthy and strong, but there's always a possibility of accident or disease to interfere with this. You may win the woman you want, and you may lose her.

There's chance and luck in everything; that is, in everything but one. You can be a Real Man if you want to hard enough, and all hell and heredity, bad luck and misfortune cannot defeat you.

Isn't it a comforting thing to know that there is one thing in the world that's a certainty? And isn't it doubly heartening to realize that this one thing is the greatest and most worthwhile thing of all things?

What is a Real Man?

A Real Man is a man who honestly tries to live up to the best he knows.

That's all. You see, it's simple. Like all the great things of life, it is plain as a pike-staff.

Just to know what is best is not enough; many a cad and coward knows, but he doesn't do.

And to feel, to realize, to appreciate, to love the best, does not imply that you are a Real Man. Many a drunkard and many a shiftless profligate is a mighty feeler.

A Real Man is one who responds nobly to circumstances. The harder the knocks and the more discouraging the situation, the brighter he shines.

A Real Man respects himself. Self-reverence comes very close to God-reverence. A Real Man has certain personal sanctities, of body, of thought, of feeling. The fine flavor of reverence is always about him.

A Real Man is steadied and sobered by responsibility and success and fame.

A Real Man is nerved and stimulated by failure and defeat. A Real Man is a good loser. He never whines. It's always up and come again with him.

A Real Man never talks about what the world owes him, the happiness he deserves, the chance he ought by right to have, and all that. All he claims is the right to live and play the man.

A Real Man is just as honest alone in the dark, in his own room, as he is in public.

A Real Man does not want pulls, tips, and favors. He wants work and honest wages.

A Real Man is loyal to his friend and guards his reputation as his own.

A Real Man is dependable. His simple word is as good as his Bible oath.

A Real Man does a little more than he promises.

A Real Man does not want something for nothing, so the get-rich-quick people cannot use him.

A Real Man honors a woman, any woman. He cannot hurt a woman, physically or morally. He sticks to his wife. He can be loyal, even if it becomes impossible to love.

A Real Man minds his own business. He does not judge other people.

A Real Man always has an excuse for others, never for himself. He is patient and charitable to them; to himself he is strict.

A Real Man is glad to live, and not afraid to die.

A Real Man never hunts danger, and never dodges it when he ought to meet it.

A Real Man is—well, he is a Real Man, the finest, best, noblest, most refreshing thing to find on all the green earth, unless it be a Real Woman.

REASON

Volume 5

It is well and good to be rational, and to have reasons for what you do, but the best things we do, those of which we are justly proudest, those indeed for which our friends love us most, are the things we do for no reason at all.

Take love, the greatest thing in the world. It is never so fine as when it defies intelligence, laughs

at prudence, mocks at consequences, and gives itself without money and without price.

One reason why women are so much more lovely than men is that they act from the woman's reason: "just because."

It's a poor lover who can tell why he loves.

Take heroism. Precisely because

it does not foresee nor count the cost it is admirable. The careful, wise man will do for ordinary occasions, but for the splendid deeds it needs a man who is a bit mad. Nathan Hale and Sergeant Jasper were not wise; they were better, they were heroic.

Take joy. The happy people are not those who can explain the grounds of their contentment; and when a body proceeds to prove he is happy you may rest assured he is worried.

Take religion. The apostle told his followers to be ever ready to give a reason for the faith that was in them, but my experience has been that those with the sincerest faith were those who were least disposed, and least skilled, to reason about it.

No, man, your intellect is not your highest faculty; you are superhuman only when you are caught in the fires of primal instincts.

The Reflex Action of Words

Volume 6

In the beginning is the Word. We commonly think of the Word as the end, the product and eventuation of a thought. It is. But, once uttered, a word has a certain reflex action, and returns to have an effect upon the speaker.

We not only say things because we think them, we also think things because we say them.

There are some who tell us to say we are well, and never to say we suffer, to assert happiness and success, and deny sorrow and failure, and it will be unto us according to our assertion. Perhaps we have been impatient at such advice and declare we will not lie nor act the hypocrite, but will honestly say what we feel and possibly we have regarded people who talk so to us as imbeciles, trying to lift themselves by their bootstraps.

But revise your harsh judgment. Go over the matter thoughtfully, and you may perceive that these enthusiasts are not wholly wrong. There is a modicum of truth in their idea. They have glimpsed the secret power of the reflex action of words.

Physically, a word is a sound vibration; it is possible to break a wineglass by a properly pitched tone. And spiritually also a word has its vibrations, and affects the mind and feeling.

We think in words, when we think clearly. For when our thoughts cannot be expressed they are quite vague and influence us not much.

We feel in words. Most of our desires and passions run in the channels that words have worn.

So there is sound psychology in saying that words can make us sick or well. Talk of your diseases and they will grow. Talk of health and you will be healthy.

It is not a matter of lying, but of selection and suppression. Search out any normal, happy, successful, healthy element in yourself—you can always find something of the kind if you look for it—and speak of that. And if you have pain, depression, fear, worry, or any sort of gloom, turn away your mind from it as much as possible, and at any

rate do not talk about it.

Your strong, bright words will fly back to you. In every one of them is a seed of feeling; it will fall within the garden of your heart and make a flower.

And if you have the yeastings of sourness and bitterness within you, at least give them not culture of words; batten them down in darkness and silence, and they will die for lack of air.

You can always keep your mouth shut. It may help you. It will certainly help us.

REST AN ILLUSION

Volume 5

Rest is an illusion. So is stability. So is permanency. There are no such things.

Many a man has worked hard nine-tenths of his life, getting ready to rest the other tenth. When he arrives at the rest period he is disappointed. He cannot rest. He doesn't know how. His last tenth is usually boredom, often rapid decay.

A common idea of heaven is that it is eternal rest, loafing forever and ever. But to an active personality the prospect of never-ending inactivity is not inviting.

When we look about us in nature we find that what we term

stability does not exist. Nothing abides. The mountains crumble. The ocean continuously alters. The stars burn up, even as the grass withers.

What we call stability is merely the equilibrium of constantly active forces. The keystone in the arch remains for centuries, not because there is no force exerted upon it, but because the opposing pushes are always balanced.

The atoms in a brick or piece of steel are in as lively motion as the atoms in a running stream.

The stars seem fixed, but really are whirling unceasingly in their courses, our own earth spinning on its axis and driving forward on its circuit with the others.

The garden mould, the tree trunk, the brooding bird, the nest egg, the motionless pond, the quiet flower, all are hives of myriad activities.

Nothing is dead. Motion is everywhere. In the solids, motion has simply retreated further into microscopic obscurity.

Let the soul, then, look for relief, not in cessation, not in annihilation, not in Nirvana or repose, but in the restfulness that comes from changed activity.

Rhythm is the eternal law. Life goes in waves. Rest is simply the trough of the fluid wave.

I shall go forward and backward, shall rise and fall, shall labor and play, shall wake and sleep, but never stop.

I am a note of the cosmic music and must go on vibrating forever.

In making plans for old age one should arrange for some sort of absorbing work. For without interesting activity old age is likely to collapse.

A workingman, angry at Dr. Eliot, president of Harvard University, wrote to him, saying that he hoped something would happen so that Dr. Eliot would have to work hard all the remainder of his life. To which the doctor replied that nothing more desirable could befall him.

RHYTHM

In all motion, as Herbert Spencer shows in a singularly beautiful chapter of his *First Principles,* there is rhythm. The wind comes in gusts, waters move in waves, the seasons rotate, night and day alternate, the lungs expand and contract, the blood circulates in beats, we wake and sleep and so on. It is the same with life's more intangible forces. Passion rises and falls, reforms advance in periods, fashions come and go, and business teeters from prosperity to panic. It would

save us a great deal of alarm if we bore this law in mind. The matter with many a wife is that she needs a vacation, not with her husband, but from him. Many a friend is lost by seeing too much of him. More than one bride has spoiled her honeymoon because she would not allow the groom to get out of her sight long enough for him to realize how happy he was. The deepest want of the human creature is Something Else. The man will chop more wood if he stops once in a while to spit on his hands. "Keeping everlastingly at it brings success"—also paresis. It does not even pay to be very, very good all the time. There was a saint, whose name is on the calendar, who said, "I went away from God that I might find Him."

THE RIGHT TO MAKE ONE'S OWN MISTAKES

Volume 1

Mr. T. Jefferson and others briefly listed the inalienable human rights as three: life, liberty, and the pursuit of happiness.

There is a fourth: the right to make one's own mistakes.

Nowhere is the deep wisdom and justice of the Creator more apparent than in his so arranging the Universe that a man can do his own sinning. We cannot understand this. We are so dazzled by ideals that we cannot see the supreme privilege of freedom is freedom to do wrong. Take that away, and a man becomes non-moral. Virtue is of account only in one who might have chosen vice.

We learn more by our own mistakes than by any other means. Let a man always succeed and he will remain a child, ignorant, egotistic, unsympathetic, and cruel. It is because the king can do no wrong that the king is usually a poor little soul.

Our growth, character, enjoyment of life come from our mistakes. A child that is not permitted to fall will never learn to walk; for walking is a succession of falls.

In our eagerness to make our children successful we rob them of the very foundation of success, which is failure; for the truest success is what is left after a hundred failures. We are so anxious to have them happy that we take from them the key to happiness, which is the privilege of making themselves and others miserable.

I want the right to burn my own fingers, bump my own head, eat indigestible food, and do the whole range of silly and senseless things. Only when I am at perfect liberty to scar, scratch, smash, and ruin my life, only then am I capable of triumph, power, and goodness.

It is important to be trained in morality; it is still more important to be trained in liberty.

Moral slumping is always easy and moral bracing hard.
—THE HABIT OF SELF-CONFIDENCE

THE ROAD TO HELL

The greatest sin against yourself is having a good impulse and not acting upon it.

The human race may be divided into two classes—the potent and the impotent. The potent use their emotions to put force into their deeds, the impotent use their emotions for entertainment.

Nothing is so injurious as to play with high ideals and not put them to work. You get so after a while that you cannot put them to work.

There are people who regularly go to church and weep and thrill and make no effort to translate their Sunday feelings into every-day activities. They are connoisseurs in sentiments. They are exquisite critics of high passions. But in their actual life they are petty, selfish, and sordid. And they are worse sinners than those who never go to church at all, who never indulge in religious ecstasies.

There are drunkards who abound in good resolutions. They are experts in the emotional part of reforming, but they never reform. They know the noble joy of swearing off, and often indulge in the fine spasms of resolution, but they go on drinking. By and by their will ceases to be steel; it becomes limp as a cotton string.

"No matter how full a reservoir of maxims one may possess," says William James, "and no matter how good one's sentiments may be, if one have not taken advantage of every concrete opportunity to act, one's character may remain entirely unaffected for the better. With good intentions hell is proverbially paved."

So there you have the road to hell. It is not refusing to have ideals and good emotions and noble sentiments; it is having them and not expressing them in action.

A sentiment must get into your motor nerves before it reacts to do you any good.

An emotion drunkard is about as bad as a whiskey drunkard.

"He who every day makes a fresh resolve is like one who, arriving at the edge of a ditch he is to leap, forever stops and returns for a fresh run," says Bahnsen.

An unused conviction not only is of no value, it does positive injury. It dulls the edge of your power of decision. It exhausts all the reserves of impulse in you, so that at last nothing at all can move you.

It is not the lack of ideals that ails the world, it is so many ideals that are not lived out. Every one of these turns into poison.

Here is the evil of excessive novel reading, theatre-going, and religious sentiment. The more we thrill, and do not, the flabbier we become.

The remedy is: never allow yourself to indulge in a good emotion without expressing it in some active way. As William James expresses it: "Let this expression be the least thing in the world, speaking genially to one's grandmother, or giving up one's seat in a tramcar, if nothing more heroic offers—but let it not fail to take place."

THE ROAD TO THANKFULNESS

Volume 5

Thankfulness is an attitude of mind.

It is another name for happiness. When one is happy one is thankful, and vice versa.

To be thankful simply means that one thinks he is better off than he deserves to be. And this leads us to the great and luminous truth that happiness is not a thing at all, but is the relation between two things; that is, the relation between our condition and what we think our condition ought to be, between what we have and what we conceive to be our deserts.

If that be so, then the road to happiness ought to lie very plain before all of us. It is, to change our thought instead of trying to change our things.

Here is the situation. My house is not fine enough, my food is not plentiful enough, my clothes are not expensive enough, my wife is not handsome enough, my neighbors are not agreeable enough, my bank-account is not large enough, and so on. Hence I am unhappy. I say I don't see what I have to be thankful for. I worry and stew and am generally miserable.

Now to cure this state of things I can proceed in one of two ways. (1) I can get me a finer house, better food, a prettier wife, more money, and the like; or (2) I CAN CHANGE MY NOTION ABOUT WHAT I DESERVE.

The first method is followed by the fools; the second by the wise.

For several reasons.

1. You can always change your idea of your deserts, and you cannot always get more and better things.

2. If you start getting more things you generally find that your opinion of your deserts rises along with them, in fact usually keeps a few leaps ahead, so that your resultant state of dissatisfaction remains constant, about the same.

The last thing the average person will admit, however, is that the cause of his unhappiness lies within himself. He is very willing to address himself to the question which forms one of Mr. Gilbert Chesterton's titles, "What's Wrong With the World," but rather resents it if you suggest the topic, "What's Wrong With Me."

For all that, the gentle reader is recommended, if he cares to find the short and straight road to happiness, to lock himself up in his room alone and whittle down his conception of what he ought to have.

He can get more happiness out of one hour's exercise at this than he can get out of a year's labor at increasing his pile of goods or improving his environment.

Regulating one's self will probably never be a popular indoor sport, but for all that it is the most profitable—much more so than regulating the universe, or the country, or the laws, or one's relations.

The road to thankfulness lies through your own soul.

THE ROOT OF HAPPINESS

Volume 5

I have," said Lady Orlay, "never known a great happiness that was not built upon the wreckage of other happinesses. That is why happy people are never gay."

In this text the root of happiness is indicated. It is sorrow.

Sadness is as essential to fulness of life as joy.

The proper aim of existence is perfect self-expression, and not a succession of mere pleasurable sensations. And sorrow is quite as necessary for the full equipment of the soul as glee.

A life without sorrows is as a picture without shadows.

All beauty is an arrangement of shadows. All charm is the play of light and shade, and all happiness is a creature of pains.

You can get no good crops unless you plough deep. And no satisfying contentment is possible to a heart that has not been cultivated by the share of anguish.

When you say you are always happy we infer that you are either shallow, or that you are forcing yourself to believe what you think you ought to believe, possibly following the teaching of some cult that inculcates pulling one's self up by one's spiritual bootstraps.

The desirable life is not all sweet; it is bitter-sweet.

Your gloomy days, your experiences of rebuff, your failures, your rainy seasons of sadness, your wistful moments, your pangs of dream and longing, they are not wasted, they are making you deeply fertile, they are preparing your soil to grow that happiness which is as a ripe, round apple; unploughed hearts grow only crab-apples.

The richest nature that ever lived was called " a man of sorrows and acquainted with grief." And out of his sorrow-drenched depths there grew a most amazing peace, so that he said to his friends:

"Peace I leave with you; my peace I give unto you; not as the world giveth give I unto you."

And not only is sorrow a prelude to joy, a preparatory state for joy to come, but it may contain in itself a certain indescribable yet very real joy, if nobly borne.

For it is well known that in practising self-denial and undertaking hardship for one we love, for instance, there is a far sublimer contentment than in self-indulgence.

Then do not look for happiness in the lighted cabarets, in banquet-halls, in the riot of amusement, and where the loud laugh echoes; go among the shadows, down life's dark lanes, where men labor and women wait, where grinding work is endured for love's sake, and loneliness and bereavement and pain are faced with courage, where the bitter waters run, and thorns are found, and look with heavenly insight, and you will find in plenty the whitest lilies and the reddest and most odorous roses of this our strange and wondrous humanity.

Said Thomas Hood in his "Ode to Melancholy":

"Then give to her her tribute just,
Her sighs and tears and musings
   holy.
There is no music in the life
That rings with idiot laughter
   only."

RUST

If anything is not used it is rusted. Physicians say there are certain diseased conditions in which the body eats itself, as in diabetes.

It is true of all parts of both soul and body that what is not properly exercised atrophies. If you do not exert your muscles they devour their own strength. If you do not put food into your stomach to digest it, it will, so to speak, digest itself.

So also the mind that does not

continually study and learn does not remain blank, but fills up with a vast mass of untruths which destroy it. Ignorance is the rust of the mind.

It is fully as hard on the system to have nothing to do as to be overworked; worse indeed to rust out than to wear out.

The soul, too, that is not actually putting forth its power deteriorates.

If you will not have faith, you shall have worry, which is soul-rust.

If you will not love, you shall have ennui and pessimism.

If you will not exercise in self-sacrifice for others, you shall be sacrificed on the altar of self, and perish in the slow fires of selfishness.

"Antisthenes used to say," writes Diogenes Laertius, "that envious people were devoured by their own disposition, just as iron is by rust."

A School for Living

What is needed in the world is some sort of school or asylum or institution or correspondence course to teach people how to live.

More than anything else they need to know that. Yet states and school systems are telling them everything but that.

Single tax is grand and socialism is alluring, women's rights are needed, dress reform and simplified spelling, food-chewing, prohibition, and criminal laws are all right in their way; but still the "one thing needful" is to know how to live.

That is what's the matter with all of us who go wrong.

Only one kind of education is of first account for a bad boy; it is the kind that educates him to live. Geography and manual training will not cure him of his cussedness, nor will common fractions and United States history help him to be clean, brave, and kind.

Here are the subjects in which a public-school pupil ought to be drilled:

How to control my temper.

How to use my imagination so as to strengthen me instead of making me weak.

How to improve and toughen my will.

How to find pleasure in common things.

How to get joy out of nature.

How to curb my selfishness and develop my altruism.

How to play fair.

How to work so as to make work a pleasure.

How to be a good fellow without being a fool.

How to get stimulation out of simple food and water drink, and not alcohol.

How to control my sex instinct so as to make it conduce to my permanent happiness and not to disease, mental misery, and the wrecking of my career.

How to make friends and keep them.

How to handle enemies and those who wrong or offend me.

How to get along with relatives and all those persons with whom I come in contact.

How to value my own self-esteem more than the praise of others.

When a man commits a crime it is simply because he doesn't understand how to live. Why lock him up in a prison where he is forced down still lower in degradation? Why not have a "how-to-live" school and send him there? And, indeed, why not send him to such a school in the first place, so that he will not become a criminal?

We even arrest a person for attempting to commit suicide, and lead him to jail, when all the trouble with him is that he doesn't know how to live, else he would not have wanted to quit.

Think of all the restless, worried,

morbid, unhappy, complaining creatures who simply need a few primary lessons in the art of living.

They think they want money, or notoriety, or to travel, or get divorced, or to change their circumstances; but these things are not what they need; they need to know how to live.

And nobody tells them. Schools don't tell them, doctors don't tell them, judges and prison-keepers don't tell them.

Millions blunder along and make a mess of life because they have studied anything else under the sun except living.

Most people have philosophies of life, ideas on the subject of happiness, and dreams of success that are cheap, absurd, and idiotic.

I have met millionaires, successful businessmen, learned professors, gifted artists, and able preachers who have not the slightest notion of how to be happy.

Yet I shall not start a school of this kind, for the simple reason that those who most need to learn how to live are the first to resent the suggestion that they need it.

Humility is the only door by which wisdom and greatness and peace can enter, and it is usually barred and bolted by pride and egotism.

True love needs no management; it manages us.

—THOUGHTS ON LOVE

THE SEED

The Seven Wonders of the World were by no means the most wonderful things in the world.

The wonders of life are thickest among the familiar, every-day matters.

Perhaps the most amazing, baffling, mysterious thing in all the universe is a seed.

Look at an apple tree. All of its trunk form, the law of its branches, its leaves and their veins, its delicate blossoms, and its fruit, were contained in a little, brown, hard seed. Open the seed and you see nothing but a whitish filling; yet that substance has powers as strange as mind, it has a plan that implies wood, flowers, and apples.

Out of my window in the morning I hear roosters giving their hoarse, peculiar call. They all sing practically the same tune. Once it was in the egg. Think of that yolk and white in the egg holding in itself the potentiality of a certain cry. And cocks crow now doubtless as they crew in the Garden of Eden.

Take two particles of vital fluid; the microscopist can hardly determine a difference between them; yet from one comes a lion, with all his complicated organism of hair, nails, blood-vessels, viscera, nerve-threads, mental tendencies, characteristics; and from the other a man with a body as complex as that of the lion, and with a brain containing the thoughts, fancies, and spiritual functions of an intelligent being.

It seems uncanny when we consider a talking-machine and observe the tones of a voice, or a piano, or a violin, or the full music of an orchestra, pass through the point of a needle. It seems impossible, a miracle.

And yet it is not so astounding as to note how a living being, a duck, a dog, an oak tree, a rosebush, concentrates all of its marvellous organism into an egg or seed, from which a similar organism is produced.

Not any of the sights of earth are comparable to the seed. The falls of Niagara, the cathedral of Saint Peter at Rome, the pyramids of Egypt, the peaks of the Himalayas, none of them is so overwhelming to a thoughtful mind as a little grain of wheat.

The miracle of miracles is life. And the seed is life's most miraculous manifestation.

The wonders of electricity, of radioactivity, of hypnotism, clairvoyance, and dreams, of the starry heavens with their stupendous masses and distances, of chemical affinity and the strange appetencies of molecules, of art and of invention, cannot, to me, compare with the seed, where there is condensed into a single, small, not very highly organized substance "all the physical, moral, and intellectual past and future of thousands of creatures."

If I were going to be a heathen man, and seek in nature some object to worship as God, some object embodying the infinite mystery of life, I should worship a seed.

SELF-STARTERS

Volume 7

What you need, man, is a Self-Starter. You go along all right when somebody cranks you up, but that kind of a machine is getting more and more out of style.

You have fine staying qualities, but poor starting qualities.

You have patience, perseverance, honesty, fidelity, and so on, but you don't seem to be able to start anything. Including yourself.

Now, good and faithful workers are needed in this world, for there's a deal of machinery to keep running, and chores to do, but there are also a lot of people to attend to such things, as they can't do anything else.

And if that's all you can do, or all you want or hope to do, well and good. I hope you'll get your due wages, be a faithful member of the party, and die in your bed.

I throw no bricks at you. I hope you'll be respected, protected, and even, upon occasion, uplifted.

But if you want to rise from the ranks, step out, and be somebody, you'll have to get you a Self-Starter.

For only the Self-Starting folks arrive at the grand show on time to get an aisle seat up in front.

I notice from your conversation that you lay a good deal of stress on luck and acquaintance and having a pull and all that sort of thing.

I'm not denying these are good things. They help a fellow get along. But the trouble is they are of value only to the man that can get along without them.

Everybody helps him who helps himself, nothing succeeds like success, and the only man everybody wants to lend money to is the banker.

So, after all, there's nothing to it. Whatever you do, you must do it yourself—you must begin, anyway.

You study too much about how to succeed, you consult other people's opinions, you are long on referendum and short on initiative.

Nobody showed Marshall Field

how to do business. Nobody was responsible for John D. Rockefeller's money except John D. Rockefeller himself. Nobody had to stand by and pat Admiral Dewey on the back and tell him to cheer up, when he went after the Spanish fleet at Manila. And nobody cranked up Mark Twain or Lloyd George.

They had Self-Starters.

Go get you one!

SHADOWS

No life can be great without the equipment of sorrow.

There is a depth of sweetness, an abiding light, in a heart that has known suffering and borne it nobly, that prosperity and long contentment cannot have.

It is sometimes bitterly said that God is the invention of the ruling classes, of the rich and favored and fat. But the contrary is the case, for belief in God is fed from the springs of trouble. "Worship," said Carlyle, "lies at the bottom of sorrow."

The beauty of the rose depends upon the muck and the dead leaves sacrificed at its roots.

Out of the battlefields of Europe is springing a strange new birth of faith.

Out of the havoc of tyranny will come a strong, irresistible movement for liberty. The only thing that can compensate humanity for the present orgy of mad dynasties is a revolution that will democratize the people and establish the United States of Europe.

Sorrow comes to everyone. And well for the soul that understands that the beauty and richness of life lie in its shadows!

When the day comes that your soul is of age, when you have arrived at last at wisdom, then you will be thankful for every rebuff fate gave you, for with the stripes of destiny you are healed.

Disappointment, disillusion, betrayal, pain, failure—every one of them is but a part of that dead manure the great Gardener has been digging in about your soul, that someday the lilies of majesty may bloom in you.

It is the shadows that make us human. It is well to be happy; but better to be human.

"The shadows!" exclaimed Auguste Rodin, as he gazed upon the *Venus de Milo* in the Louvre, that incomparable masterpiece of human achievement. "The divine play of shadows on antique marbles! One might say that shadows love masterpieces. They hang upon them, they make for them adornment. I find only among the Gothics and with Rembrandt such orchestras of shadows. They surround beauty with mystery. They pour peace upon us."

"No man could have amassed enough treasures of feeling to transform the world by his life and words, no man could have pushed humanity up to divine kinship, except "a man of sorrows."

SIN

Volume 5

Susannah Wesley, mother of John, was, from all accounts, a remarkable woman. She had a dozen or so children and sense to match.

One day, for instance, a neighbor, amazed at the quiet patience of Mrs. Wesley, asked: "Why do you tell that child the same thing over twenty times?"

"Because," answered she, "nineteen is not enough." But it is another saying of the great Susannah upon which we now design to animadvert.* To wit, namely, a sentence from one of her letters to her son John who wanted to know exactly what sin is. His mother told him, and in these words: "Would you judge of the lawfulness or unlawfulness of pleasure, take this rule: Whatever weakens your reason, impairs the tenderness of your conscience, obscures your sense of God, takes off your relish for spiritual things—whatever increases the authority of the body over the mind—that thing is sin to you, however innocent it may seem in itself."

I do not know that I have seen anywhere, in or out of books on theology and ethics, a better and a more understandable definition of sin.

Everybody wants to know what is right and what is wrong, the lax as well as the virtuous; and much of the wrong-doing of the world arises from confusion of mind. Sin lies not all in the warped will.

And if everybody would lay Susanna's words to heart, and, to use a phrase of John's, "read, mark, learn, and inwardly digest" the same, 'twould save us from many a moral muddle.

And if you can't master it all, or possibly don't approve of it all, just take a part of it—those words, "whatever increases the authority of the body over the mind, that thing to you is sin."

I think it was Amiel—or was it Joubert?—who said that all culture consisted in transferring our pleasures from the body over to the mind, so that the arts and sciences are the handmaids of religion.

*note

But the chief excellence of this excellent woman's dictum is her emphasis upon the fact that sin is personal. It lies not in the infraction of any code or rules, but in our inward cowardice and moral flabbiness, in our disloyalty to our own conviction, in our refusal to follow our sense of Ought.

SLOVENLY THOUGHT

Volume 7

Clean up your thought.

Don't have your mind looking like the dining-table after a banquet, or the floor after a political meeting. Sweep it and dust it, and put the ideas away where they belong.

Don't have a waste-basket mind.

Or a top-bureau-drawer mind.

It doesn't do you much good to have a grand idea, or a wonderful impression, or a strong passion, if you don't know where to put it.

I notice when I talk to you that you have a good many interesting notions. The trouble is they are all higgledy-piggledy; they have no unity, coherence, order, organization.

You think, but you don't think anything out. Your wheat is full of chaff.

Perhaps I can help you if you will lend me your ear for a space.

1. Don't pick up some opinion you hear, and make it your own because it sounds fine, and go to passing it out, without carefully examining it, scrutinizing, cross-questioning, and testing it.

2. One of the best tests of any opinion (not an infallible, but a very valuable test) is, "Will it work?" If it won't, something's wrong with it, nine times out of ten. That last brilliant notion of yours—hundreds of sensible people have had it, and discarded it, because it wouldn't work.

3. Don't let anybody make you think you owe a certain amount of belief in a thing simply because you can't disprove it. Nor be deceived by the argument, "If that doesn't account for it, what does?" You don't have to account for it at all. Some of the most pestiferous bunk has got itself established by this kind of reasoning. You don't have to believe or disbelieve everything that comes along; most things you just hang up and wait.

4. Don't be afraid to say, "I don't know." It's a sign that you know what you do know.

5. Ask questions. Don't be ashamed of appearing ignorant.

What you ought to be ashamed of is seeming to understand when you don't.

6. Classify. Education is nothing but the art of classification. Keep a scrapbook. Keep an index rerum. And classify.

7. Waste no time in acquiring "general information." Always read and study with a purpose. Look up subjects; don't just read books. Books are to be referred to, consulted, not to be read through—that is, as a rule.

8. Be a friend and daily companion to the dictionary and encyclopedia.

Look things up.

9. Define. Practise defining. Practise telling what a thing is not, as well as what it is.

10. Get a clear idea of what you don't know. Then you can see better what you do know.

11. Write. Not for publication, necessarily, but for yourself. Writing accustoms you to choose just the right words. Beware of adjectives, especially two of them. Favor nouns. Use simple, short words. They mean more, and carry further.

12. And never hurry or worry.

SOMEBODY IS FOLLOWING YOU

Volume 4

Somebody is following you. Somebody sees your footprints in the sand and is unconsciously going your way.

Somebody is catching a glimpse of you as you thread your way through life's mysterious woods, and is coming after you, perhaps merely because he knows no better direction to take.

Thackeray said that no Irishman was so poor that he did not have a still poorer Irishman living at his expense. And nobody is so insignificant and commonplace that he does not determine by his example the life of someone else.

We are fond of underrating ourselves, to escape responsibility. But the fatal power of leading others is unescapable. They follow us whether we will or no, and often the more persistently in such measure as we have no wish to be followed.

For the examples most doggedly imitated are of those who do not set themselves up as examples.

When a man cries, "Do not as I do," then his manners take strongest hold on us.

It is not the great models of conduct and piety that grasp us; it is the little every-day models of negligence.

The boy swears and goes dirty to be like Huck Finn. The little girl melts into the mould of the silly and simpering miss. The youth drinks because others drink.

People do things because others do, more than for any other reason.

This is the strange force of crowds, where we are swept along by the cumulative power of example to do what in our sober judgment we would never have done.

A little of this pulling power rests in every one of us. No matter how small and inconsiderable a person you seem to yourself to be, someone is being led by you by the invisible towlines that reach out from you to him.

No soul walks alone.

No act of self-restraint or of petulance is without an echo in someone.

Down the ways of life you walk at the head of some sort of a procession. Dimly and instinctively they follow you.

Unconsciously, even more than consciously, you are making this world a better or a worse place, you are adding to its pile of happiness or its heap of misery, you are shedding light or spreading gloom.

You cannot help it so long as you live.

When the final books are balanced it is your "little nameless unremembered acts" that will weigh most.

SOMETHING TO LIVE FOR

Volume 4

Living is not much fun unless you have something to live for.

Bread is the staff of physical life; an aim is the staff of spiritual life.

Without some goal, some object toward which your thoughts, energies, and hopes bend, your life gets flabby. It also gets either cold and useless or fevered and poisonous.

By and by you hate yourself. And others are inclined to make it unanimous.

Man is not an independent animal.

He is by nature dependent. He is essentially social. When he tries to go it alone, to be sufficient unto himself, he goes crazy.

There are some people who are unbalanced because they have taken up some absorbing ideal, such as religion, or patriotism, or moneymaking, or music. But for every one such there are twenty who are warped, morbid, and lopsided because they haven't any ideal at all.

"Hitch your wagon to a star," said

the philosopher. If you don't hitch it to something it won't go.

What shall I live for? You can answer the question by another: What is worth dying for? When you've found the thing worth dying for you've found the thing worth living for.

There's more stimulus in a great aim than in any other intoxicant. It raises every faculty of you to the highest power. It clears your brain, fills your heart, and raises your happiness to flood tide.

Do you notice how happy the child in the house is when he is made to realize he has something to do; how happy the man when he feels that a family depends on him for support; how happy the woman when she sees that she is essential to some man's or children's happiness?

In all this horror of world war there is a kernel of joy. The bitter plant has borne at least one sweet fruit. Nations, and the millions in them, have found something to die for, hence to live for.

In a recent book, *From the Human End*, by L.P. Jack, a distinguished Oxford professor, it is stated: "The war has brought to England a peace of mind such as she has not possessed for generations. That element of 'poise' in life which

Matthew Arnold valued so highly has become an actual possession of millions in whom twelve months ago it was utterly lacking. It seems a strange phenomenon, and yet it is nothing more nor less than the peace of mind which comes to every man who, after tossing about among uncertainties, finds at last a mission, a cause to which he can devote himself, body and soul. At last he has something to live for, and though the living may be hard and costly he makes no complaint; all that is well repaid by the harmony that comes from the unitary aim of his life."

Thousands in the United States feel the same. To numberless young men the donning of the khaki means a certain ennoblement, an enrichment of life. By taking a great thought we have added a cubit to our stature.

A deep thrill is informing* many a life that until now was full of self-contempt. The aimless young man is beginning to understand the dignity and glory of a soul, who,

> "If he be called upon to face
> Some awful moment to which
>   Heaven has joined
> Great issues, good or bad for hu-
>   mankind,
> Is happy as a lover."

Pride is a comfortable sensation. But its price is a fall, which is not comfortable.
—PAY, PAY, PAY!

*direct; give character to

SORROW ENLARGES THE HEART

We all run after pleasure and away from sorrow, and yet it is pleasure that corrodes us and sorrow that strengthens us.

No worse fate could befall a human being than to have his lot so cast that every desire would be gratified. Give him abundant wealth, the satisfaction of every physical instinct and every day full of happy surprises, and it would not be long before he turned upon himself like a mad tiger in its cage and began eating his own heart. Tannhauser at last could not endure the lap of Venus, and out of his sensual heaven cried out for a taste of some of the agonies of his fellow-men, as Dives in hell pled for a drop of water.

It is sorrow, in truth, that is the basis of joy. Without sorrow a palate is dulled, and we become unable to taste joy, as a man who dines luxuriously every day becomes indifferent to food, and as after a period of starvation he realizes the exquisite flavor of dry bread.

Only by going down into the pit where there is no pleasure at all do we come up with a sharpened sense that is capable of detecting the myriad shades of satisfaction, which they who have never suffered cannot appreciate.

The soldiers who are now fighting in France are undergoing privations and are exposed to dangers they would never have met had they stayed home. Yet there is no doubt that they are having a richer and fuller life. They are finding joys they would never have suspected had they stayed at home on the farm or in the grocery-store. Hardship is unveiling for them another world, of high and perilous beauty, a world into which few adventure of their own accord, but in which, when once Destiny has ushered us there, are unfolded the diviner and more heroic sensations of the soul.

All human experiences have two sides. There is a black and bloody side of war, and there is a shining side. This terrible time in which we live is like the sad and often discordant music of "Tristan and Isolde," from which the naïve ear shrinks, but which, when once we have come to understand and appreciate it, shows us the exquisite reaches of sensation in sorrow which joy can never rival. Even of the terror of these times we may say, with Edmund Gosse:

> "But when that true, fierce music—
>   full of pain,
> And wounded memory, and the
>   tone austere
> Of antique passions, fills our hearts
>   again,

We marvel at our light and frivo-
lous ear."

So a great poet said: "The plea-
sure that is in sorrow is sweeter than the pleasure of pleasure itself,
and hence the saying, 'It is better to
go to the house of mourning than
to the house of feasting.'"

THE SPIRIT OF THE DAY'S WORK

Volume 7

Perhaps we might get along better if we remembered that it is
all in a day's work.

There's a lot to be done, but we
don't have to do it all today.

And the higher the task, and the
more difficult, delicate, and important the matter, the more necessary
it is to attack in the spirit of a day's
work at a time.

To learn to play the piano, or to
read French, or to overcome a bad
habit, or to write shorthand, or to
achieve poise, and patience, or to be
good—nobody can come at such
accomplishments at once.

It is little by little, the steady
forcing of the will upon one's
stubborn desire, mind, or fingers,
whether we feel like it or not, just
as a day's work, it is so we crawl up
the steep hill of perfection.

The will to do is important, and
the ambition to do is necessary, and
hard work counts; but one essential
to any excellence, whether in craftsmanship or character, is time.

Somehow or other the past en-
dues us. There's no such thing as a fresh start. Every new start carries
with it something of those we made
before. Every effort silts something
into our nerves or muscles or brain
cells so that they are different next
time.

The power of the thirtieth day is
the result of the invisible dividends
of the twenty-nine preceding days'
work.

Somebody asked Susanne Wesley, John's mother, why she told her
children the same thing over and
over twenty times. "Because nineteen is not enough," she answered.

In that greatest of earthly busi-
nesses, mothering, it is the spirit of
the day's work that helps. To carry
on so complicated and vital affair
as the training of children there is
needed above all that self-posses-
sion which comes only when we
conceive of our work as lasting but
one day. And it is when we look
forward too much and keep expecting results that time alone can give,
that we fall into the petulance or
fretfulness that destroys the quality
of our guidance.

The clock has millions of tick-tocks to make, but it has a moment in which to do each one of them. The sun rises regularly to his duty, and sets at night satisfied with what increment of growth his day's work has supplied to living things.

And we—we need never expect to arrive—our business is not to arrive, it is to travel, to cover each day our allotted span, leaving all questions of ends and values and rewards to that Mind that thinks in centuries and weaves men and the labors of men into its vast fabric.

Our plan is on the trestle-board, our lines are known for this day's duties, let us do what is marked out for us; it is for us in this world to live "by the day," and not "by the job."

SPIRITUAL DIGESTION

Volume 5

The soul as well as the body has a digestion.

And as it does not make much difference what you eat so long as you can digest it, so it does not so much matter what happens to you, but it matters a deal how you can transmute events into thought.

I know a young man upon whom fortune seems to have rained her cruelest blows. Death has robbed him of one he most loved. A swindler took away his money. Finally paralysis has deprived him of the use of his limbs. He cannot walk. He sits all day at his window. If anybody has reason to take the advice of Job's wife and "curse God and die," it would seem to be this youth.

Yet his is the brightest eye, the cheeriest smile, I know. Young companions love to come and sit with him in his room; he is the life of any company. It is a treat to see him play cards; his interest is so lively in the game, though someone must handle his cards for him.

His soul simply has a wonderful digestion, that takes all the whips and stings of an outrageous fortune, and they become joy and radiance in him.

And there are some in whom all the beauty and shine of this pleasant world are turned to gall. In a sketch by Reuben Sacks is depicted such a one. See what bitter stuff this woman makes for herself in the crucible of her mind!

"It seemed to her, as she sat there in the fading light, that this is the bitter lesson of existence; that the sacred serves only to teach the full meaning of sacrilege; the beautiful of the hideous; modesty of outrage;

joy of sorrow; life of death."

That there are such disordered spiritual stomachs in the world is pitifully true. Nothing can so outrage a Pharisee as a gentle radical like the Nazarene.

There are men who grow meaner, crueler, and more vicious, the sweeter and gentler their wife strives to be.

There are children whose insolence increases with the kindness shown them.

There are dyspeptic souls to whom sunshine is an indecency and rain an insult; goodness is hypocrisy; enthusiasm to be sneered at—whatever thought gets into them turns sour.

For such we can have but pity. They are "notes all out of tune in this world's instrument."

Their worst victim is themselves.

Yet alas for those who love them!

Theirs is hell; for the undeniablest of hells is dyspepsia.

Such are the sad ones that pass the suicide way. What bitterness must have gone before the hour where death was preferable to life!

Such a one was Amy Levy, the English poetess, of whom Thomas Bailey Aldrich wrote:

"A girl
That with her own most gentle desperate hand
From out God's mystic setting plucked life's pearl—
'Tis hard to understand.
So precious life is! Even to the old
The hours are as a miser's coins, and she—
Within her hands lay youth's unminted gold
And all felicity."

THE SPIRITUAL VALUE OF PICKING UP AFTER ONE'S SELF

Volume 8

There are still, let us hope, some old-fashioned people left who are anxious to save their children's souls. That is, while they would like them to get on and get rich and be prominent, they would much more like them to be clean, strong, honest, and happy. The latter class includes the saved; the former most of the damned.

And to such parents, of wholesome and sane mind, I would say:

If you want to save your child's soul, teach him to wait on himself and to pick up after himself.

There is no one thing in this world more destructive to Christianity—nay, I will go further and say more destructive to the spirit of humanity—than being waited on and picked up after.

The very essence of that sweetness

and light which constitute the shine of greater souls is the indwelling desire to be of help to others.

And, conversely, the very core and gist of that devil-spirit that makes about all the trouble on earth is the desire to have others help me.

This baneful desire takes many forms and has many names. It is called selfishness, and disrupts families. It is called thoughtfulness, and severs friends. It is called pride, and stubbornness, and causes wars. It is called greed, and works all manner of tort and cruelty. It is called vanity, and tramples on every graceful flower of life. It is called ambition, and sacrifices on its bloody high altar every dove and lamb of human contentment.

But under whatever masquerade it goes it is always the same constant desire to have somebody else do things for me and to avoid doing things for somebody else.

The laws of the spirit as are unerring and inevitable as the laws of matter, and the effect follows cause in the soul's business with as steely precision as two and two make four, or fire and gunpowder make explosion. And the persistent aim to make other people minister to me will bring me sorrow and dryness of soul, and the dominant wish to minister to others will bring peace and deep joy in life, just as surely as any logical sequence in mathematics.

Hence, begin early, if you care for your child's life.

No matter how rich you are, nor how many servants you can afford, teach your boy, as soon as he is able to learn, how to be sufficient for his own physical needs; how to dress himself, polish his own shoes, keep his own nails clean, take his own bath, sew on his own buttons, empty his own slops, keep his own room and bureau-drawer in order, hang up his own clothes, pick up his own playthings, and never leave dirt or confusion after him.

Let your little girl learn, at the very earliest age, how to brush her own hair, to care for her own linen, to mend her own frocks, to darn her own stockings, and to cook her own food as far as practicable.

Real Christianity and real democracy amount to the same thing, and that thing is: To keep yourself off other people's backs.

If we had learned that we would have no spoiled and rotten smart set whose concern is clothes, amusement, sex-excitement, and intoxication.

If we had learned that we would have no endowed class, consisting of useless leeches living on the blood of workers.

We would have no kings, nobles, millionaires, and aristocrats, nor any of that class of magnificent ones from whom flow the never-ending streams of oppression, fraud, wretchedness, poverty, and war that make this fair green earth a stinking Gehenna.

If you want, most of all, your boy to be famous or rich, you needn't bother. But if you want him to be a man, a joy to himself and to all that shall have to do with him, teach him only to be of as little trouble as possible to servants, parents, and playmates.

If you want your daughter to get the best price for herself in the market of adulation, it doesn't matter. But if you wish her to be a cease-less source of love and strength to herself and to all hearts that shall touch hers, teach her "not to be ministered unto, but to minister."

THE SQUIRREL

Volume 4

One summer morning, in At-lantic, Iowa, I rose early from an uncomfortable bed in the hotel, and went out into the little park that is in the central square of the town. There I sat under the trees beside a fountain and saw the dawn shimmer.

A little squirrel ran up to me, stopped, sat up, cocked his head, eyed me a minute and scampered away. Nothing could exceed the exquisiteness of his motion. His progress was a series of graceful un-dulations; he ran along the grass as a wave runs along the sea. Arched back and flowing tail were perfect curves.

What a bundle of finely wrought nerves and muscles, what a little masterpiece of life from the hand of the most skilled of all artists, Na-ture!

And yet, I reflect, smitten by the plague of thought: to what purpose is all this workmanship? What was he made for? What will be his end? Some day, doubtless, to fall a prey to a cruel enemy, somewhere at last to lie and decay and give back all his marvellous machinery of fur and eye and throbbing heart to the rust of the earth and the gasses of the air. Beasts and birds, flowers and pretty girls, all this living jew-elry, Nature wears but a day or so, and then throws it back into her laboratory to make new joy-things to deck herself withal.

For all that, every creature seems to be happy, except the human creature. He alone has the fatal gifts of memory and apprehension. He alone breaks the heart of the present between the upper and the nether millstones of the future and the past. The other animals drink the cup of joy when it is passed; our stomachs are dyspeptic with too much tomorrow and yesterday.

If the soul could only let itself sink into the perfect beauty and health and gladness of the present, it would taste the bliss of Nature's children.

Of course we must plan and we must regret. It is the backward look and forward look that make us great. And when occasion requires let us take up the burden of this tragedy. But as a habit of life, as an exercise for the better part of every day, let us sink into the wonder and beauty of what is, and not wear forever the suffocating garments of what was and what will be.

When death comes to the squirrel it is usually sudden death, which is the best kind. He never feels it till he meets it, and the pang is not long. It casts no shadow on his life.

And for us mortals it is not death, but "the valley of the shadow of death," that clouds life.

THE SUNNY SIDE OF THE HILL

Volume 9

I live," said a friend, "on the sunny side of the hill."

Why not? Every hill has two sides. It may be a long way around to the other one, but it's there. Move! Why live in the gloom?

Early in spring the peach-trees are blooming on the sunny slope, while on the other the soil is still cold and backward. Their blossoms laugh to the sky. There is fragrance and beauty on the sunny side.

Every condition into which we get has two sides. No matter how dispiriting it is, somewhere it has a face whereon the light falls. Let us look around until we find it.

Only this view of the cloud is dark. Above, the sun pours on it, it is white and bright. Come, let us fly over the clouds and not always live beneath them.

You have no flying-machine? Oh yes, you have. Imagination is one wing of your airplane, and faith is the other, while the powerful propeller is courage. Learn moral aeronautics.

Every man, every woman, you meet has a sunny side. Nobody is totally impossible. With the use of a little self-control and persistence you can discover a side to everyone where he shines a bit with agreeableness.

Love is a great sun-finder. Look at some of the men that women love!

And selfishness and pride are the prize gloom-finders. A selfish person always moves on the north side of people. Such a one would find fault with the music of Israfel or the looks of Aphrodite.

Every event that happens has its sunny side. There is a shrewd and wise way to take any failure or disaster, any sickness or bereavement. Not hard stoicism, but gentle faith, I mean.

There is a Buddhist tale of a dead dog, lying by the roadside. Many passed and expressed their aversion. Then came the sage, and as he looked upon the repulsive object he remarked:

"What beautiful teeth!"

SYMAPTHY

Volume 9

"In a highly civilized society," said Rabbi Samuel Schulman the other day, "we are more and more in danger of losing our sympathies."

A soul's sympathies are its riches. The poorest man in the world is the one who has lost his power to feel for others.

Sympathy is the cement of mankind, and holds the race together. All forms of selfishness, including greed, cruelty, and luxury, are isolating.

If all people had perfect sympathy, there would be an end to unjust conditions.

When some artist strikes a chord that makes the hearts of the world vibrate in harmony, and that strongly appeals to the imagination of a nation, the reform is already won.

The Bitter Cry of Children, "The Song of the Shirt," and *Uncle Tom's Cabin* did more toward alleviating the wrongs they referred to than any laws or armies.

"Make us feel; make us feel!" cries the multitude. "We do not want to be taught; we want our hearts moved within us."

We advance only by the development of our imagination. It is the story-teller, the poet, the orator, that urges us forward. "The eternal feminine leads us on."

The things that clog universal sympathy are class and system.

Emerging from the savage state of individualism, the world learned its first steps in sympathy through class. First there was the family, then the allied families or tribe, then all sorts of limited brotherhoods, such as churches, unions, associations, lodges, clubs, and the like, then the nation, and at last the world consciousness.

It is all a widening of our power of sympathy. By that the world comes to itself, finds itself, is organized, unified, and saved.

For civilization means sympathy.

The danger of class sympathy, confined to members of our own organization, is that it tends to stop there and be satisfied with itself; also that, in order to preserve and intensify our brotherly sentiment among ourselves, we cultivate a hostility toward other groups.

System also, in increasing our efficiency by classifying us into groups, tends to narrow us.

But labor and capital, for instance, are never going to solve their difficulties and prosper by developing hates, by fighting, but by developing their mutual sympathy, by learning to understand each other and to join hand in hand.

If our sympathy were highly active, we could not for a moment endure that huge armies and navies be kept prepared for contingent slaughter, that little children should be forced to work to minister to our needs and pleasures, that crowds of unemployed men every winter besiege our cities, and that the products of land and labor be so distributed that the few live in abundance and the many in dwarfing penury.

We are dull, cold, heartless. Our prayer is ever for some new Prometheus to bring down spiritual fire from heaven and heat up the commandment, "Love thy neighbor as thyself."

Ten Success Hunches

Volume 7

A very human letter lies before me. "I read your editorials daily," says the writer, a young man, "and have been especially interested in those that touch upon ambition and opportunity.

"Now I would like you to answer me just one question. What is a young man to do when he reaches the age of twenty-one with no special training? He has lots of ambition, besides ability to work, but he finds that this talk about courage and will-power is nothing but rot. For wherever he seeks an opportunity to start from the bottom no one pays attention. The very men who preach opportunity and rising to high position in life by hard work refuse to make a place for him. They tell you about using your brains, but at the same time they don't give you a chance to use them.

"Can you explain how in the world there is any opportunity in such a case?"

Well, in the first place, living all those years until twenty-one without training is a crime. But perhaps it was not your fault. If you ever have children, however, see that you do not wrong them as your parents and the state, and possibly yourself, wronged you.

Still, at twenty-one you have the world before you. Perhaps these hints may help you:

1. Don't be impatient. It's a life job you're tackling. Set your jaw. Plan for years, not for tomorrow only.

2. Remember that your real success takes place inside of your mind. It's not facts, nor others' acts, nor events, that matter. Nothing matters in the long run but the temper of your spirit. Keep thinking success; and the more you are rebuffed the harder you must think it.

3. You seem sorry for yourself. That looks bad. Flee thoughts of self-pity as you would the devil. Are you alive and kicking, and have you a clear head and two good hands, and are you out of jail? If so, you're in luck.

4. Study. I'll venture to say you waste enough spare time in four years to make a doctor's degree. Find out what you want to do. Say it's engineering. Take up a course of study in that direction.

5. Do well what you can find to do. Do it with all your skill and enthusiasm. Do it better than anyone else can do it. Do it—and keep your eye open for something better. Be efficient. Every factory, store, and farm in the world is hungry for the man who can do the business and not make excuses.

"Creation's cry goes up
From age to cheated age;
Give us the men who do the work
For which they get the wage."

6. Don't fret. Don't worry. Have faith. Believe in yourself. Believe in the world. Believe in the Eternal Justice. If you do, the stars will fight for you. And if you don't believe, if you complain and get it into your head that this world is down on you, why, it will come down on you and smash you, and you'll get what you believed in. Everybody does.

7. Be persistent. Fortune's a fickle jade. If she does not say yes the first five times you ask her, ask her twenty-five times. After a while she will favor you, for she loves importunity.

8. Get the luck idea out of your head. There is such a thing as luck. But that is not what you are looking for. What you want is success. And there's no luck about that. It's just as certain as the corn crop to those who know how to raise it.

9. Don't expect anything of anybody but yourself.

10. And keep cheerful. It's all in a lifetime. Meanwhile there are doughnuts and coffee. And the pleasant sun

in shining. I suspect you are missing a lot of happiness because you don't know it when you see it.

Do you remember what Lincoln said?

"I have noticed that most people in this world are about as happy as they have made up their minds to be."

THE THINGS NOT SEEN

———————————————————*Volume 8*

Over and above and behind and within the things seen are the things not seen, and they are most important.

So much more vital are they that a great thinker said, "We look not at the things that are seen, but at the things that are not seen; for the things seen are temporal, but the things not seen are eternal."

For instance, the house is a thing seen, but a home is a thing unseen; a brain can be seen, a mind is unseen; you can see a mother's face, but not the love behind it, yet it is the latter that affects you; flags are seen, patriotism unseen; and you can see a body, but not a soul, a word, but not an idea, a church, but not God.

Our first crude notion is that the things seen are real and the things not seen are fanciful. We call those who handle stone and wood and meat practical, and those who deal in sentiments and morals, theoretical.

Sometimes we hear one say that he goes in for the tangible goods of this life, such as food, clothes, and money, and he prides himself upon his sound common sense.

But the truth is that what is seen is mostly illusion. The earth seems flat; it is not, it is round. The sun appears to revolve around us, but we revolve around it.

What we call education is but the process of correcting the false ideas we get from things visible by the things invisible. The baby, who can see as well as we, is continually bumping himself against the things seen until he learns how to use his judgment, reason, and other unseen faculties.

It is the unseen things that matter. So true is this that the Hindu philosophers speak of all the things we see as Maya or Illusion.

Behind every tangible thing look for the intangible, which is more solid and essential. For it is not lust you need, but love; not money, but abundance, which is a spiritual substance; not clothes, but self-expression; not bread, but truth; not beautiful objects, but a mind that can see beauty anywhere; not an amulet, but courage; not wine, but health and enthusiasm.

Why are you unhappy? Because you are hungry. You put material food every day into your stomach and you drink water, but you do not draw into your inner man, into your real self, the boundless supplies of the infinite. Love, joy, peace, mirth, and all the good vital forces are about you, as the atmosphere is about you, but your spirit's mouth is shut tight, because you are stupid and vain, and think you are clever, in that you will only believe what you see.

If you would be happy, come, buy without money and without price; eat and let your soul delight itself in fatness, for the infinite storehouse is yours, and the humblest soul may revel in its unseen treasures.

THOUGHTS

Volume 5

How much pleasure do you get from your own thoughts? As a matter of fact, do you not hate them? Are you not in the habit of running away from them? When you are left to your own resources, are you not bored, wretched, and lonesome? You have studied how to strengthen your memory, how to train your reason, how to cultivate your imagination, and all of that; did you ever address yourself to the simple question of how to enjoy your mind? What a wide world is the thought world! The empire of Great Britain, upon which the sun never sets, is a small spot compared to it. For your thoughts embrace not only this planet but all the stars; they roam through Europe and Patagonia, from ancient Babylon to future Utopia.

How quick and supple they are! They beat Puck in his flight around the earth. I can think of Julius Cæsar, and in a trice he disappears and is replaced by Lord Kitchener.

Past and present mean nothing to my thoughts. Everything is now. Now are the huge flying lizards of the days before man existed, now Lucifer falls his nine long days from heaven to the pit, now Alexander's legions roll through Mesopotamia, and now Cromwell's Ironsides stand against the king. No moving-picture show can equal my thought show.

Is it not singular that a creature with a power like this should become bored and sigh for something to amuse him? Is it not strange that we so dread to be left alone with our thoughts, left alone with this thought machine that is at once magician, miracle-worker, cinematograph, phonograph, and winged Mercury?

In me, in my mind, are all things. As I lie in bed, there, in my pillowed head, swarm stars, clouds, oceans, deserts, men, women, books, events. For me it is not things themselves that exist, it is the thoughts of things.

And are not thought-goodness and thought-sin even deeper than outward deeds? A sin committed is bad enough, but by openness is already half-cured, while foul and wicked thoughts, nursed in the mind, poison the whole character. And if you can only sit and think of kindness, courage, and beauty, you are doing much to help along the world.

NO THOUGHT IS EVER LOST. THE DYE OF IT STAINS THE UNIVERSE.

A love thought without the deed is better than a love deed that is not born of thought.

"Life," says Marcus Aurelius, "is what our thought makes it"; and the appeal of Holy Writ is, "Let the unrighteous man forsake his thoughts."

THOUGHTS ON LOVE

—Volume 2

There are some who think the absence of love to be a virtue, and who speak of "the crimes of love." But there can be no virtue that is not love's forthputting; there is no vice that is not love's denial.

Love is hot, and heat is life; it creates heaven. Hate is cold; it creates hell. Dante said hell is cold.

Only one love is true and great; we are gods but once.

Only the impotent sneer at love.

Love is an art, not a science. We can be taught a science; we learn an art by trying.

In the realm of the highest life values, we do not buy and sell; we give and receive. Love cannot be deserved.

There is no taste of death in the mouth like dead love.

When love dies we die; from then on until we are buried we only exist.

True love needs no management; it manages us.

Love excuses everything—among men. Passion excuses everything—among brutes.

The highest love is a thing of destiny and has its cause somewhere in the stars.

Love is the eye of the soul. Coldness is blind.

Though love is essential to life, there is a hidden instinct in the heart of every man and woman to destroy it.

Sin is not purged by prayer, fasting, and self-mutilation, but by love.

The only dangerous heretics are those who doubt love.

Only the wise can know; only the skilled can do; but the least and lowest can love as an archangel.

In love lies our common divinity.

One who loves me is my best priest.

As soon as woman thinks herself less loved she makes herself less loveable.

It is singular that a woman is so charitable toward the man who would ruin her, and so exacting toward the man who worships her.

The mind ever seeks perfect truth; the heart, perfect love; and both quests lead beyond the grave.

God made the world for lovers; all others are intruders.

No man finds himself until he loves a woman.

There is no justice without love, no understanding without love, no growth without love.

It is impossible to have permanent human relations without love. Every law founded on self-interest is a curse. The ruin of capital is its lack of love. The labor movement will never succeed without love. National affairs must always result in destruction until they begin to recognize love, the love of races instead of their rivalries.

The cure of the criminal is love.

Love is the form which evolution takes with the appearance of mankind on earth.

"The Immortal Being manifests himself in joy-form," say the sacred books of the East. (Anandarupamamritam yad vibhati.) Love is the supreme joy-form.

The soul of man is journeying from chaos to law; and the road is love.

TIME

Old Father Time knows more than anybody.

He solves more problems than all the brains in the world.

More hard knots are unloosed, more tangled questions are answered, more deadlocks are unfastened by time than by any other agency.

In the theological disputes that

once raged in Christendom neither side routed the other; time routed them both by showing that the whole subject did not matter.

After the contemporaries had had their say, time crowned Homer, Dante, Wagner, Shakespeare, Whitman, Emerson.

Almost any judgment can be appealed, but from the decision of time there is no appeal.

Do not force issues with your children. Learn to wait. Be patient. Time will bring things to pass that no immediate power can accomplish.

Do not create a crisis with your husband, your wife. Wait. See what time will do.

Time has a thousand resources, abounds in unexpected expedients.

Time brings a change in point of view, in temper, in state of mind which no contention can.

When you teach, make allowance for time. What the child cannot possibly understand now, he can grasp easily a year from now.

When you have a difficult business affair to settle, give it time, put it away and see how it will ferment, sleep on it, give it as many days as you can. It will often settle itself.

If you would produce a story, a play, a book, or an essay, write it out, then lay it aside and let it simmer, forget it a while, then take it out and write it over.

Time is the best critic, the shrewdest adviser, the frankest friend.

If you are positive you want to marry a certain person, let time have his word. Nowhere is time's advice more needed. Today we may be sure, but listen to a few tomorrows.

You are born and you will die whenever fate decides; you have nothing to do with those fatal two things; but in marriage, the third fatality, you have time. Take it.

Do not decide your beliefs and convictions suddenly. Hang up the reasons to cure. You come to permanent ideas not only by reasoning, but quite as much by growth.

Do not hobble your whole life by the immature certainties of youth. Give yourself room to change, for you must change, if you are to develop.

"Learn to labor and—to wait!"

All show of force is a sign of weakness. Loud talking is a sign of consciousness that one's reasoning is feeble. When one shrieks it means that he knows or suspects that what he says does not amount to much, and it irritates him.

—ALL NOISE IS WASTE

TO LIVE IS TO FIGHT

Volume 3

Fight! Fight! Fight! That is the law of life. Man is a fighting animal. He is also a fighting soul. Only by incessant conflict is life possible. Peace is the precursor of death. When we cease to have daily struggle we are beginning to fade. To stop is to go backward. All souls float in a stream whose steady current sets toward death. Life is to the swimmer.

The body that has ceased to overcome, to joy in triumph over ease, to leap and plunge and go, has settled down with the door open to every disease. The mind that shrinks from effort, that reads only what is spiced and pleasant, that does not love to tackle hard problems and sweat over enigmas, is moribund.* The soul that no more struggles and suffers, that finds no more passions to wrestle with, no more discouragements to surmount, is already half lost.

Every day, to a healthy being, is war. And in ratio as we are sound and sane, we love it. "To him that overcometh will I give the crown of life." As we are more and more invaded by the hunger for comfort and rest and quiet, we settle down into the waiting arms of death.

Blow on blow, the buckling on of the harness, the chase and ardor of the game—woe to the man that has not some spot in him where such taste lingers! For to live is to fight. To struggle no more is to die. "Vivre, c'est triompher sans cesse," says Amiel—"To live is to triumph continually."

THE TRUTH IN ADVERTISING

Volume 7

Listen, young man! The cleverest man in the world is the man that tells the truth, and tells it all the time, not occasionally.

Sometimes you can profit by a lie, but it is like dodging bullets; you never know when you are going to get hurt.

Lying is a game. Sometimes it is a very exciting game. But it is essentially gambling. And gambling, any sort of gambling, is not business.

The fundamental laws of business are just as accurate and as well established as the principles of geometry.

It is hard to see this, for our visual range is limited. Most of us can see the crooked dollar coming today,

*dying

but not the ten straight dollars it is going to lose us tomorrow.

Real business success is cumulative. It grows like a snowball. And the one thing that makes it keep us growing, even while we sleep, is our persistent truthfulness and dependableness.

If you put an advertisement in the paper announcing goods worth five dollars for sale at two dollars, and if the people come and buy and find out the stuff is not worth ten cents, you may make a one day's gain, but you have alienated a lot of indignant customers and have started to saw away the posts that sustain your reputation.

If you have a store rented for a week only and purpose to conduct a sacrifice sale of goods that will make everybody disgusted who buys them, then perhaps you may lie with a high hand and a stretched-out arm.

But if you are in the town to stay, and want regular, returning, increasing, satisfied, and friendly customers, it will pay you to stick to the old-fashioned truth.

Exaggeration is lying. It does not take long for the people in the community to get the habit of discounting twenty-five percent of all you say.

If you continually overstate and vociferate you must keep on getting louder, until you soon become incoherent.

But if you habitually state only what is soberly, honestly true, by and by everything you say will be away above par.

A man's repute for truthfulness is as much a part of his capital as are his store and stock; so much so that he can raise money on it.

As civilization progresses, business becomes more and more an affair of credit, of trust. The very foundation of big business is trustworthiness. Therefore, if you are ever going to get beyond the peanut-stand and push-cart stage of merchandise you must establish a basis of dependableness.

There is not one thing in this world, young man, that can be of as much value to you as building up a reputation such that men will say, "your word is as good as your bond."

It is well to be clever and keen and Johnny-on-the-spot, it is well to look out for number one and to know a good bargain, but best of all is to have the world say of you:

"Whatever that man says can absolutely be relied upon."

The needed lesson in life is to learn how to meet and
deal with danger, and not how to avoid danger.

—MORALITY WRONG END TO

The Ultimate Resource

Volume 8

You must have something in your life that does not depend upon anybody else.

If you would have your happiness secure, the root of it must be within yourself.

This is not a doctrine of selfishness, but of self-defense.

Much of our happiness is necessarily bound up with other people; it is the result of our human relationships. Companionship is that which tempers laughter, play, and work, and is the essence itself of love.

Very many of us never get beyond this range of joy. We are incapable of any pleasure that is not communal. We shudder at solitude. We flee ourself as the prince of boredom.

But those who would be secure against the shocks of existence, who would feel that they are rooted deep enough to withstand the blasts of time and circumstance, must discover themselves.

They must have some ultimate resource that the world cannot touch.

Some people find this in their vocation. Some in their avocation. Some discover it in the fruits of their imagination. Some find it in religion.

One thing is sure. The strong soul, the hero for whom nothing is tragic, the well-poised life which no untoward event can thrust into panic, is that one who has learned that the deepest supplies upon which the soul feeds, the most inexhaustible and wholesome supplies, are those that lie within himself.

In the scorn of the world, in isolation, contempt, and hunger, he can turn to fate with a smile and say, "I have meat to eat that ye know not of."

The Unconquerable

Volume 10

Reporters in the war-smitten countries of Europe tell us that one effect of the horrors of death, wounds, and heartbreak is that the men are turning back to the churches. Out of the obscene muck of materialistic force is springing a revaluation of the spirit in man.

Man is a curious animal. He seems to give forth his finest product only when crushed. We expect him to "curse God and die," and suddenly his face lights up with the heavenly vision.

We loathe poverty and fight disease and avoid wounds, tyranny, and oppression. Yet, somehow only when these come, do the rarest flowers appear on the human bush.

I know a young man, twisted, crippled, paralyzed, unable to feed or dress himself, yet who sits daily by his window with a shining face. He is cheerful, helpful, a fountain of joy to all who know him. The boys love to gather in his room at night and play cards and tell stories. One would think he would be a gloom and a burden; he is an uplift. You soon forget his limitations. You soon cease to pity him, for he does not pity himself. He does not drain you; he inspires you.

In how many another family is the sickroom the shrine of the house. How many a stricken invalid woman is the resting place for her worried husband, the delightful refuge for her children's cares!

It is not the strong, wealthy, and powerful that always gleam with optimism and radiate hope. Too often the house of luxury is the nest of bitterness, boredom, and snarling. Petulance waits on plenty. Luxury and cruelty are twins. Success brings hardness of heart.

The world could get along without its war lords, millionaires, and big men, with all their effective virility, better than it could do without its blind, deaf, hunchbacked, and bedridden. Some things we get from the first group, but the things we get from the second are more needed for this star-led race.

Little girl, with twisted spine and useless legs, with eyes always bright with golden courage, with heart ever high with undaunted love, we could spare all the proud beauties of the ballroom or the stage better than you.

Their bodies are finer than yours; but then we are not bodies.

What a strange and strangely magnificent creature is man! And how proud his Maker must be of him, for all his faults! You cannot crush him. Put him in prison and in its half-light he writes a *Pilgrim's Progress*. Strike him blind and he sings a *Paradise Lost*.

When Beethoven died, a post-mortem examination showed that since childhood he had suffered from an incurable disease, aggravated by improper medical treatment and by want of home comfort and proper food. His liver was shrunk to half its proper size. He always had family troubles that annoyed him beyond endurance. His finest works were produced after he was deaf. And this was the majestic soul that was unparalleled master of music, whose art was immeasurable, will be immortal! Yet we have heard fat artists whine because they are mistreated!

What a piece of work is man! Too wonderful, too unconquerable, too divine for this earth! His home must be among the stars!

The Universal Blunder

The universal blunder of this world," said Phillips Brooks, "is in thinking that there are certain persons put into the world to govern and certain others to obey.

"Everybody is in this world to govern and everybody to obey. There are no benefactors and no beneficiaries in distinct classes. Every man is at once both benefactor and beneficiary. Every good deed you do you ought to thank your fellowman for giving you an opportunity to do it; and they ought to be thankful to you for doing it."

That is a mighty good sentiment to set down on your tablets. It may gain you a deal of happiness if you will believe it. It may even save your soul.

Certain people work for me and I pay them wages. But the maid who sweeps my room is no more my servant than I am hers. Because I give her money and she gives me work does not make me her superior.

It is the ancient delusion of the centuries that labor in some ways lowers a man. The real fact is that it ennobles him.

For instance, Mr. Wilson is considered by the American people, and I am sure he considers himself, as their servant. He has no mortgage on his job. He holds it by no divine right. He cannot pass it on to a successor of his own blood or choice. When we don't like what he does we criticize him. There are certain partisans that yelp at him every turn he makes, like a pack of yapping pups. We do not suppress them. It is the constitutional privilege of vulgar people to scold their servants.

And yet he is the chief man of the greatest nation in the world. In former days he would have shouted, "Off with his head!" when anyone crossed him, and would have worn a crown, also a robe with a tail ten feet long. It is the spirit of service that makes him the decent, conscientious, hardworking man he is.

The curse of wealth is that it destroys this spirit of service. The man who does nothing because he has enough to live on comfortably is no better than the man who does nothing because he can beg or smoke his pipe on the bench by the poorhouse door. Both are leeches. They are not serving. They are being served.

When you lose sight of the duty of serving, you invite at once spiritual microbes of the most destructive character to come and breed in you.

There is a luxury in being waited on. But that feeling induces pride, meanness, selfishness, the undisciplined will, the unruled passions, and the whole rakehelly crew of traits that cause excess, perversion, indolence, selfishness, boredness, and pessimism.

There is a luxury, too, in serving. It is a real pleasure when it becomes a habit. It brings on the genuine happiness-makers, which are humility, unselfishness, sanity, health, optimism, cheer, and a wholesome interest in life.

The greatest of men said of himself: "The Son of Man came not to be served, but to serve."

THE UNWORKED MINE

The unworked mine is yourself. You have hidden in you unknown treasures.

On the surface you may look barren- nothing but sand and rocks. Others passing by may think you uninteresting. You may think so yourself.

You say:

"I am commonplace. I am good for nothing. I have no character, no force, I can do nothing excellently. I see this genius play the violin, and that one sing, and another build, and another amass money or speak eloquently or write charmingly, but my hands are trifling. I am next to impotence.

"A is beautiful, B is strong, C is learned, and D is famous. But I—I am nothing."

Well, many had gone over the ground and despised it, until one day Stratton dug there and found one of the most amazing goldmines in the world.

Dig!

How do you know what's in you until you dig and see?

In you is power. It may lie deep. You have never touched its vein. It will stay there unsuspected and useless until you die, if you don't dig for it.

In you is beauty. Every soul is beautiful—somewhere. Down there within you is loveliness, charm, a wonderful, divine order and symmetry. It is worth searching for. Dig!

In you is wisdom. There is no real wisdom outside of you, none that will do you any good. It is within you. You can find it in the long hours of silence when you seek among the caverns of your soul. You can find it, gems of it, like diamonds, lying in the ledges, if you use diligently the shovel of meditation.

In you is goodness. The granite rocks that underlie every soul are good. Go after what is in you. There are peace and contentment and righteousness and loyalty and love. They are all within you. Dig!

And there is God. There is heaven itself. Did not the wise one say, "You shall not say, Lo, here! nor, Lo there! For the Kingdom of Heaven is within you"?

How can I come at it? Dig! Seek, and ye shall find.

No books, no teachers, no events can give you what you want, unless you work your own mine.

The answer to the starry sky is the infinite within you.

Dig!

You will find within you riches and force and passion and joy.

For these are mixed in the clay of all souls. And He who made man's body out of the dust of the earth mixed strange treasures therein.

The Uproar

Volume 9

Violence is the greatest of Impotence. Brutality is the outward sign of inward Cowardice.

Loud talk indicates lack of conviction.

The persecutor is not quite sure of himself. It's the half-doubt [that] lights the fagot.

When the boy passes the graveyard at night he whistles, because he is afraid of being afraid. It is the same with all who vociferate.

Only those who believe with their whole hearts can keep still.

The screaming reformers do not believe their cause—wholly.

If the Germans had been absolutely sure of the superiority of their Kultur they would have left it alone, to conquer the world by its inherent excellence. Because they were not sure, they went to war.

"Defenders of the Faith!" Ludicrous title. For real faith needs no defense. It is a defense.

You don't need to stand up for the truth, and to fight for it, and to preserve it against the enemy. When you talk that way it shows you don't understand the quality of truth.

Truth is the one indestructible, evergreen, eternally persistent thing on earth.

All we have to do is to see it, to believe in it, and to adjust our lives, thought, and speech to it, and wait. By and by it always wins.

Hence genuine believers in the truth do not "strive nor cry, neither is their voice heard in the street." They are quiet, calm, glad. They have hold of the one thing that cannot fail.

They lean against the pillars of the universe.

The infinite flows through them, and they smile at the contortions of the finite.

Whoever is sure is undisturbed.

All fret, worry, apprehension, and morbidity arise from uncertainty. Those who fight are not quite sure.

Only those who are sure can afford to turn the other cheek.

Only the sure can afford to forgive their enemies.

Few reach the dizzy height of Jesus, who saw the truth so clearly, and believed so utterly in its triumph, that He refused to struggle for it.

The most amazing thing about Him was His leisureliness.

So true it is that "he that believeth shall not make haste."

Most of us have only caught up with Joshua; we are miles from Jesus.

We juggle His texts, but have no idea of His vast, calm spirit.

Let us find the truth, even if it be only the truth about wood, or metal, or mathematics, just any little piece of the truth, and believe it, and adjust ourselves to it, and be happy; for out of truth flows peace.

THE VOICES

Volume 2

V'eran genti con occhi tardi e
    gravi,
Di grand autorita ne' lor sembi-
    anti,
Parlavan rado con voci saovi.
        —Dante, *Inferno*

"There were folk with slow eyes
    and grave,
With great authority of pres-
    ence,
Who spoke sparingly with voic-
    es suave."

Teach your child how to use his voice. If he becomes expert in that, few things will be of more value to him.

His voice, more than anything else, expresses his personality and indicates the power of his moral inhibition and the degree of his culture.

Teach him to speak low. A high voice is not only disagreeable, it is a mark of weakness. Those who are sure do not raise their voices.

A high voice signifies petulance, and petulance means pettiness. The best way to stop a quarrel is to pause, take a long breath, and let the pitch of your voice down about three tones. When you begin again you will find that the heat has gone out of your dispute. What began as a contention has become a mere difference of opinion.

Teach your child to talk slowly, not to let his tongue run before his thought. This he can do if he will accustom himself never to speak until he has clearly worked out in his mind what he is going to say.

Teach him to wait. In any group of conference or consultation you will notice that the man who speaks last carries the most authority.

Let him discipline himself so that when an idea pops into his head he does not hasten to present it at once, but holds it in leash and keeps it in readiness to utter at that moment and juncture when it will have the most force.

Teach him to speak distinctly, to get into the habit, even in ordinary conversation, of enunciating every consonant distinctly, never to mumble or fill his speech with ums and ahs.

A pleasant voice and a way of speech that is agreeable to hear will carry a man far. You do not want your child to be a pedant or a sissy, to be over-nice, or disagreeably proper; but you do want him to have the manner of superiority and the air of a gentleman.

"And a gentleman," said Lord Chesterfield, "is never in a hurry."

THE WATCH, THE CLOCK, AND THE DRUM

Volume 9

Somebody said that if a watch, a clock, and a drum are going at the same time, you hear only the drum.

Stop the drum, and you hear the clock. Stop the clock, and you hear the watch.

When one denies the existence of the finer voices of life, what it usually amounts to is simply that he does not hear them, they are drowned out by coarser noises.

In the play "Sinners," a girl who has yielded to the lure of the city and sold herself for money and fine clothes happens to meet again the lover of her youth, a manly country doctor. He discovers her infamy, but instead of upbraiding her he quietly says to her, in substance: "When you get through, and turn from your present life with loathing, come back to me. Of course, I cannot love you as I once did. But I love you. I am the kind that love but once. There will never be anybody but you." And the amazed and shattered woman cries out, "I didn't know there were such men!" It is the way of us all. We do not know there exist beautiful, toweringly divine souls right among us. We do not know they walk the streets like tall white angels. We do not know they are silently doing their life tasks, close to us, so close we brush by them daily, going about their work with such stellar poise, and with so wondrous a dignity, that if we could perceive it we might hear a command from the white sky: "Put off thy shoes from off thy feet, for the place whereon thou standest is holy ground."

The drum! It sounds in the newspaper; the roar of scandal, murder, politics, and business; and obscures for us the real life of the people moving toward justice, love, and truth, but moving silently, as the watch ticks.

The drum! It rattles and throbs in war's wild clatter; but that is not all that is going on in Europe; you cannot hear the steady clock-ticks of advancing democracy, the watch-ticks of humanity marking the unfolding of men's conviction,

silent and irresistible as time.

The drum of the city! Its street-roar, its night revelry, the roll of its day traffic, its heartlessness and brute bellowing! We cannot hear the modest tickings of thousands of gentle hearts marking time to duty, to service, and to conscience.

The drum! In the bickering of the family we overwhelm the hidden music of love and loyalty, we miss the myriad thoughts of helpfulness and self-sacrifice, and we imagine they are not.

The drum in your own brain, the cheap beating and resonance of minor issues, of pride and hate and struggle—because of this you know not anything of your real life flowing in continuous undercurrent.

Stop the drum! Stop the clock! Listen to the watch! Enter into silence! You will hear deep, miraculous things, in the world, in the lives of those about you, in yourself.

For the significant processes of destiny are not as the drumbeats, but as the ticking of the watch.

THE WAY OUT

Volume 2

To get self-respect I must do those things that bring my approval.

I never approve of myself unless I do what I know I ought to do.

Self-respect, therefore, goes back to morality. When I am moral I respect myself. When I am immoral I despise myself.

If you ask what I gain by being

good, by doing what is just and fair, I answer: I gain my own self-respect.

This means happiness, the very foundation of all happiness; for without a feeling of self-approval any other pleasures rest on a basis of concealed wretchedness.

Many people are gloomy, restless, pessimistic, and profoundly miserable, and do not know why. It is because they do not respect themselves.

I am an eternal companion of myself. I am the one person I cannot get away from. If I despise this me with whom I am doomed to live all my days, how can I be content?

How, then, can I have self-respect?

The answer is simple. In every moment of my life I am called upon to decide whether to do this or that. Life is a continuous choosing. If I make it an invariable rule to choose to do that which I feel I ought to do, I will be guided into the way of peace.

To do right is the path to happiness. If you stop to think you will see that this is not "just preaching"; it is plain, psychological truth. There isn't any way to be comfortable with anybody else unless you are comfortable with yourself.

Suppose, therefore, you pause, amidst your soul-writhings and mental torments and tangled beliefs and distressing unbeliefs and dark moods and the general spiritual stew you are in—just suppose you pause and say:

"There are a million things I don't know, but there's one I do know. I know enough to do right, and I'll do it. Life is a mystery, but the feeling that I ought to do this thing and ought not to do that is no mystery, but plain as a pikestaff. I will simply begin immediately to do what I know I ought to do."

That is THE WAY OUT.

I don't know by what ways it will lead you, but I know whither it will certainly lead you—to self-respect.

And only where self-respect is do we find those two jewels of our heart's desire—peace and poise.

WHAT IS A LOST SOUL?

———————————————————————— *Volume 3*

We use the word "Lost" in several senses.

Grandmother has lost her spectacles. They are upon her hair, but she cannot find them. In this sense lost means simply misplaced.

We may have lost an opportunity, a day, a bargain, in which case we refer to what we might have had, but missed.

We may lose life or limb or money, signifying that something is no longer in our possession.

But what is meant when we speak of a man's losing his own soul?

One's soul is one's self, and one cannot lose one's self except in a figure of speech. The little girl spoke accurately who, when asked if she was lost, replied: "No, I am not lost; mamma is lost."

The real significance of the saying that one may lose his own soul is that the soul may lose its health, and consequently its happiness; in other words, that it may drop from a normal condition into abnormality and perversion.

In plain English salvation is mental, spiritual health; damnation is spiritual sickness. In the one case the soul is sound, sane, enjoys good digestion, is vigorous in its motions, and joyous in its world, as are all healthy beings. In the other case it is full of fevered fears, sickly nauseas, pains, and spasms.

Those who find their pleasure in chambering and wantonness, in drunkenness and cruelty, in other words all whose end is the gratification of the physical demands, are simply ill.

Their souls are ill. They correspond to those Georgia crackers who eat clay, to the small child who sucks her thumb, to opium-smokers, and to all those unfortunates who are driven to gratify cravings that destroy health.

A normal appetite differs from an abnormal in that it promotes those pleasures that are permanently pleasurable.

All abnormalities produce those pleasures that itch, irritate, burn, and torment.

What we term moral actions are simply those which the experience of the race has demonstrated to result in unreacting pleasure. They have no reaction of diseased disgust.

Of course the best souls have their suffering and tragedies, but they are only outward, they never affect the inward, essential peace, poise, and health-joy of the soul.

Jesus was "a man of sorrows," but He said, "My peace give I unto you," and that He came that our "joy might be full."

So no soul can be lost by anything the world can do to it; only by what it can do to itself.

The implication in Ibsen, Oscar Wilde, and Bernard Shaw, and the whole run of latter-day preachers of unmoralism, to the effect that quite as much harm may be done by good as by bad people, is merely confusion of thought. They do not distinguish between that pain which is redemptive, purifying, and deepening to human nature, and that pain which is the diseased product of human nature gone wrong.

Rest assured, morality is based on fact, just as surely as chemistry. Nobody invented it. Nobody will explain it away.

Says one of the clearest thinkers of our time: "Moral duty consists in the observance of those rules of conduct which contribute to the welfare of society and of the individuals who compose it. These rules, like the other so-called laws of nature, are discoverable by observation and experiment. Some thousands of years of such experience have led to the generalizations that stealing and murder, for instance, are inconsistent with the ends of society. There is no more doubt they are so than that unsupported stones will fall."

The soul that does not believe this is lost. That is to say he is as sure to lose his soul's health as he would by regularly eating impure food be sure to lose his bodily health.

WHAT IS A SOUL?

———————————————————————————*Volume 8*

Referring to what you said some time ago about the soul," writes a correspondent, "I would respectfully ask: What is the soul? Where is it located? How do you know you have a soul? To say that the soul is the immortal part is dodging the question. Is there any real proof that there is anything except material substance, or body, to a human being?"

To the inquiry, "What is the soul?" we must honestly say, "I don't know."

It should be added, however, that because we do not know what a thing is constitutes no reason why we should not talk about it and use it.

As a matter of fact, the most usable, practical things in the world are things whose essence and real nature we understand least.

Take electricity, for instance, one of the most serviceable forces extant; it pulls our trolley-cars and railway-trains, gives us light and heat, communicates thought signs, heals diseases, and does all manner of every-day work for us; we know how to generate it, how to turn it on and off, what substances will conduct it; we can measure its power; we can do almost as much with it as we can with wood or iron; and yet nobody in all the world knows what it is.

Nobody knows what gravitation is, though it grips all creation; nor chemical affinity, though it pertains to every molecule of matter; nor love, though it is the biggest factor in life.

When we use the word soul it is really by way of expressing our conception of what a human being is. If he is merely a lump of highly organized and sensitized matter, if his motives and acts can be determined by the same sort of reactions that take place in the chemist's retorts and test-tubes, then he is only a body. But if he is a mysterious, inexplicable phenomenon, wholly different from all other creatures on earth, because he thinks and has notions of right and wrong, then he is more than another kind of animal, he is more than a perfected anthropoid ape, he is —we do not know what, and we call him a soul to express that "added something."

To use the term soul therefore implies that we conceive of man as a creature who functions in ways that cannot possibly be explained by chemistry, or by any laws that operate in stones, trees, or animals.

We do not know that man is immortal; we believe it, but it is essentially unknowable. Immortality, therefore, cannot be proved in the way that such knowable things as mathematics can be proved, but it can be believed.

And the best, the most valuable, the most indispensable things in life are not the things we know , as that two and two make four, but the things we believe, as that your wife loves you, your friends are loyal to you, or that doing right is better than doing wrong.

It is this belief of the dignity, worth, and importance of human life that redeems the world from baseness and gross animalism.

Metaphysicians have quarrelled for centuries over what "reality" is and what "truth" is. One of the cleverest tests of truth is that given by those called "pragmatists," of whom the late William James was the leading exponent. They say that the best test of truth is, "Will it work?" And judged by this test surely no idea could be more truthful than the soul idea, for none exercises a more practically useful influence upon individual and communal life.

WHAT IS EFFICIENCY?

What is efficiency? It is doing things, not wishing you could do them, dreaming about them, or wondering if you can do them.

It is the power to learn how to

do things by doing them, as learning to walk by walking, or learning to sell goods by selling them.

It is knowing how to apply theory to practise.

It is the trick of turning defeat into experience and using it to achieve success.

It is the ability to mass one's personality at any given time or place; it is skill in quick mobilization of one's resources.

It is making everything that is past minister to the future.

It is the elimination of the three microbes of weakness—regret, worry, and fear.

It is self-reliance clothed with modesty.

It is persistence plus politeness.

It is the hand of steel in the velvet glove.

It is alertness, presence of mind, readiness to adjust one's self to the unexpected.

It is sacrificing personal feelings to the will to win.

It is impinging the ego against the combination of events—luck, fate, custom, and prejudice—until they give way.

It is massing the me against the universe.

It is the sum of the three quantities—purpose, practise, and patience.

It is the measure of a man, the real size of his soul.

It is the ability to use one's passions, likes, dislikes, habits, experience, education, mind, body, and heart—and not to be used by these things.

It is self-mastery, concentration, vision, and common sense.

It is the sum total of all that's in a man.

WHAT RELIGION IS

Mr. E. H. Southern, in his account of his experiences with the Young Men's Christian Association in France, says that one of the stated demands of that organization is "Men who inspire by service and not convert by argument."

In this sentence is epitomized the tremendous change which religious propaganda has undergone within the last few years.

At last religious organizations are realizing what religion is.

When you get right down to its actual substance, it isn't a creed, it isn't a mode of conduct, it isn't ethics, it isn't a feeling, although it involves all these things.

It is personal influence.

It is the radiation of personality.

True religion is the forth-putting of a person dominated by the highest virtues, such as love, mercy, truth, and courage. It makes men human. False religion is the influence of them that are ruled by arrogance, selfishness, cruelty, and fanaticism. It makes men inhuman.

While creed makes some difference, as a man's opinion necessarily affects his character, and to believe a non-fact is always septic, its importance has in former ages been exaggerated.

Christianity is simply the personal influence of the Christ type of man; it is the perpetration of the personal influence of Jesus.

Christianity has spread because men fall in love with the Christ kind of people.

All the money, endowments, temples, armies, Defenders of the Faith, arguers, organizations and institutions of Christianity have been, in the long run, liabilities and not assets.

The real assets, the real conquering forces, of this religion have been the dynamic radiations from Christlike lives.

The YMCA has had this truth thrust upon it. It has been wise enough to take. That is the reason it is receiving a more universal support than any other religious movement in civilization ever had.

Jesus went about doing good. He healed the sick, fed the hungry, made the blind to see and them that mourned to rejoice. He formulated no creed, held no revivals, organized no church, state, or army.

He just shone.

And when the YMCA men (and this, of course, includes similar organizations) pass doughnuts and coffee to tired soldiers, provide recreation huts, give entertainments, furnish cigarettes and writing-paper, and altogether cheer and comfort those who are standing between civilization and its destruction, and when they don't argue and try to convert men and impose some formula of belief on them before they help them, they are doing about what Jesus would do.

Service through the YMCA and the Red Cross, that is the new challenge of Christianity to the world.

And the beauty of it is that it doesn't anger anybody or arouse any opposition. Jews, Mohammedans, Skeptics, and Agnostics smile and say Godspeed.

In service there is no contention.

Life is a continuous choosing. If I make it an invariable
rule to choose to do that which I feel I ought to do,
I will be guided into the way of peace.

—THE WAY OUT

WHAT TO DO

An interesting letter comes to me from a man who says that he has had enough of my finding fault with this, that, and the other in society, in law, and in customs; that he is aweary of this aimless iconoclasm; and that he wishes that I would come out flat-footed and tell him and the world precisely what to do to remedy the injustice and folly of mankind.

I could comply with his requests. I or any other opinionated man could in a half-hour tell the world just what it ought to do.

"I can call spirits from the vasty
deep.
Why, so can I, or so can any man;
But will they come when you do
call for them?"

The trouble lies here: that neither the individual man nor mankind in general becomes better by TELLING.

Didactic teaching may do some good, but only in a very roundabout way; by familiarizing the hearer with helpful principles and ideas.

If an angel from God were to appear and tell the world precisely what to do, and if every man and woman believed him, they still would not, and could not, do what he said.

The reason is a psychological one. It is that the net result of any truth you hand a man is the product of that truth MIXED WITH THE STUFF ALREADY IN HIS MIND. Your information is not ADDED to his, it is DILUTED by his.

It all depends on the kind of mind, the whole set of ideas, habits, temperament, and so on with which the imparted truth is compounded.

Hence we see that progress is a matter of growth; it is slow; it moves by waves a generation apart. Old notions and inborn prejudices die hard, and rule us a long while after they are dead.

But justice, truth, and reason must eventually live down error.

The human mind today is haunted by a swarm of ghosts of ancient frauds. Think how many people today still believe in the divine right of kings, in the "natural" right of inheriting property, in the supremacy of Mahomet, and that criminals can be cured by punishment!

"Some day," said Victor Hugo, "children will be amazed to hear that there were kings in Europe." And some day, we may say, children will look back with incredulity upon our own era, where mothers can be content with their happy children and not turn a hand to rescue the myriad other children from stunting toil.

Many a thinker has thought out

an elaborate plan for smashing things and composing them all anew. But not so comes the Golden Age.

It is a tree growing, not a house building. Age after age things get better, as the long rising of the tide.

Truth is like a lump of leaven which a woman puts in a measure of meal "until the whole is leavened."

All we can do is to keep on declaring the truth as we see it; putting in the leaven and waiting. We are digging about the truth, watering and cultivating it. We do not "make" it; the gardener does not "make" apples.

WHEN TO INSURGE

Volume 2

It's all right to be resigned, to take things as they come, and not complain; but there are things which we ought not to accept smilingly, against which we ought to kick strenuously, and protest loudly.

"When it rains," says James Whitcomb Riley, "why, rain's my choice"; and this is a sample of intelligent resignation. To the thermometer and the barometer you should adjust yourself. When you accidentally break your leg, there is nothing to do better than to look pleasant and try to think it is all for the best.

When death separates us from our beloved, when the market goes down at the moment that we expect it to go up, when old age comes, when the hour-hand on the clock moves, and when the sun goes down, we are face to face with the inevitable.

But there is a world of other conditions in the presence of which cheerful adjustment is little less than a crime. There are certain events of which to say, "The Lord's will be done!" is blasphemy, when it is not cowardice; for it would be much more honest to say, "The devil's will be done!"

For instance, to begin at home, the unruly, spoiled, petulant, self-willed and selfish child, who rules the house by sheer force of disagreeableness. This is no case for pious resignation.

There are the bullying husband and the nagging wife and the mischief-making neighbor. Here what you need is spunk, not sweetness and forbearance.

When you climb over the end-seat hog in the street car, the righteous thing to do is not to move softly and apologize, but, quite by accident, of course, to drive your heel into his pet corn.

When your city is owned and run by a gang of grafters it is time to arise and smite.

When shrewd thieves manipulate the world of business so that stock that is pure water is made to pay 16 percent dividend, while the workers' wages are reduced, that is no time to be praying to be content in the position in which Providence has placed you. You have not been placed by Providence, you have been flimflammed by rascals.

When streets are unswept and backyards are unclean and alleys vile with rubbish, and the pest comes along and begins work upon the children, that is no time for fasting and prayer, or for kissing the rod. It is time to blow the horn and summon the troublemakers to battle.

Submission to the unavoidable is good, but submission to the devices of wrong, crafty, cruel, or lazy people is contemptible.

"We make the greater part of the evil circumstances in which we are placed," said Southey, "and then we fit ourselves for those circumstances by a process of degradation."

A man who is always satisfied, calm, and equable, who does nothing but smile and smile in this world where villainy is far from extinct, is either a fool or a knave. Every decent man ought to get angry about once in so often, just to maintain his self-respect.

What Tolstoy Said about World Martyrs

Volume 1

Let me ask the novelists, dramatists, poets, and all them that show us mankind as it is, one question. I have seen the bitter, tragic thing you call Life. I have tasted its salt and sickening flavor in Ibsen, Sudermann, George Eliot, Maupassant, and Zola. I have heard its moan in Wagner and Debussy and Puccini. I have seen its sadness in Israels, Millet, Piloty, and Stuck.

My question is this: What would befall a man who would simply follow the spirit, teachings, and example of Jesus?

He would have a hard time. But would it be harder than your people have?

It is difficult to live according to Jesus. But is it any less difficult to live according to yourself, or anyone else?

The Jesus life is impractical. But is it any more so than a non-Jesus life?

Suppose a man turned the other cheek, renounced wealth and place, lived to serve and not to rule, to make others and not himself happy. You say he would be devoured. But are not those who live just contrary to this program also devoured and miserable?

You assert that the Christ life is an "iridescent dream." But is not the life of the men and women of the world a dream, and not even iridescent, but drab and troubled?

"Go through your great cities," writes Tolstoy, "and observe the distorted humanity found therein, the suffering, the violent deaths and suicides, and then ask yourself the cause of all this, and you will find that the majority of persons are martyrs to the doctrine of selfishness and sensuality, the opposite of the doctrine of Jesus."

Compare the two: World martyrs and Christian martyrs.

What You Are When You Are Not Trying Is What You Really Are
Volume 1

What are you when you are not trying? That is what I want to know. You may be able to play the piano, or to converse brilliantly, or to deliver a stirring oration, or to write a thumping story, or to make a clever business deal, or even to be good, when you gather all your forces and hurl yourself at it. But when you let go, and are not straining to do anything or be anything, and you don't care, and your coat is off and your slippers on and your feet are up and the fire crackles merrily and there's nothing to do till tomorrow, then I'd like to meet you and converse and hear you unburden your mind. For it is only when mind and body quit and rest that the soul comes out for an airing. In moments of relaxation personality emerges. What you do, by effort, is mostly a compromise; it may be partly yourself, but the greater part is composed of conditions of the material you work with and the rules of the game. Other people, luck, the favor of heaven, and even weather enter into your studied deeds. Your successes are but a small part yours. For your failures doubtless you are but little to blame. But for yourself, neither success nor failure, just your own personality as it is, you are responsible. That is what I love, if I love you. What you do or say makes little difference, unless it be what you say or do carelessly. Let me hear you swear, or whistle or hum, or let me see you play with a child, let me observe your unchecked impulse run, and I shall know you. In the day of judgment it is for our idle words that we are held accountable.

WHERE TO TAKE HOLD

—————————————————————————————*Volume 4*

The place to take hold is Here. Right Here.

And the time to begin is Now. Right Now.

If you don't know how to go at it right, go at it wrong, but go at it.

All the worthwhile things of this life are difficult. Nothing's easy but slumping.

Most of the problems that affect your happiness are complicated.

And the way to perform a difficult and complicated task is to go to it—somehow.

For you learn by trying.

Life is an art, not a science. It is mastered by experiment, and patience, and infinite beginnings again. Nobody in the world can learn just what to do before he does it; I mean in the way of living and getting along.

If you have to see a man, and dread the interview, because he is an impossible fellow and will make things as hard for you as he can, go right away and get it over with.

If your desk is cluttered with a dozen half-finished matters, clean it up now. Decide. Act.

If you owe money, pay it. If you cannot pay it, make the best arrangements you can with your creditor now. Don't evade and equivocate. Don't dawdle.

If you have a lesson to learn at school, and it looks formidable, and you don't see how you can possibly master it by tomorrow's class, go at it, learn a little of it now, get what you can of it, only don't wait for some miracle to happen.

If you have a bad habit that is throttling you, take hold now. You must conquer it sometime, and every day you delay your fight your enemy grows stronger.

If you want to save money and get a little ahead, put a portion of what you have now in the savings-bank. Nothing is finished that was never begun.

If you really want to be charitable and help your fellow-man, give of what you now possess.

If you are not helpful with a dollar only in your pocket, you would not be if you had a million.

Do it now.

What you are going to do some day may be a sickly dream. It's what you do today that means something.

The only theory that is of any value is the one that gets into your fingers right now.

The only creed that will save your soul is the one that flushes your heart and thought and speech and deed now.

The place to take hold is Here!

YESTERDAY

Volume 7

I am Yesterday. I am gone from you forever.

I am the last of a long procession of days, streaming behind you, away from you, pouring into mist and obscurity, and at last into the ocean of oblivion.

Each of us has his burden, of triumph, of defeat, of laughter, of bitterness; we bear our load from you into forgetfulness; yet as we go we each leave something in your subconsciousness.

We fill your soul's cellar.

I depart from you, yet I am ever with you.

Once I was called Tomorrow, and was virgin pure; then I became your bride and was named Today; now I am Yesterday, and carry upon me the eternal stain of your embrace.

I am one of the leaves of a growing book. There are many pages before me. Some day you shall turn us all over and read us and know what you are.

I am pale, for I have no hope. Only memories.

I am rich, for I have wisdom.

I bore you a child, and left him with you. His name is Experience.

You do not like to look at me. I am not pretty. I am majestic, fateful, serious.

You do not love my voice. It does not speak to your desires; it is cool and even and full of prudence.

I am Yesterday; yet I am the same as Today and Forever; for I AM YOU; and you cannot escape from yourself.

Sometimes I talk with my companions about you. Some of us carry the scars of your cruelty. Some the wretchedness of your crime. Some the beauty of your goodness. We do not love you. We do not hate you. We judge you.

We have no compassion; only Today has that. We have no encouragement for you; only Tomorrow has that.

We stand at the front door of the past welcoming the single file of days, that pass through, watching Tomorrows becoming Todays and then enter among us.

Little by little we suck out your life, as vampires. As you grow older we absorb your thought. You turn to us more and more, less and less toward Tomorrow.

Our snows cumber your back and whiten your head. Our icy waters put out your passions. Our exhalations dim your hopes. Our many tombstones crowd into your landscape. Our dead loves, burnt-out enthusiasms, shattered dream-houses, dissolved illusions, move to you, surround you.

Tomorrows come unnoticed. Todays slip by unheeded. More and more you become a creature of Yesterdays.

Ours are banquet-halls full of wine-soaked tablecloths, broken viands, wilted roses.

Ours are empty churches, where aspirations were, where only ghosts are.

Ours are ghastly Pompeiian streets, rich galleons a hundred fathoms deep, genealogical lists of sonorous names, mummies in museums, fragmentary pillars of battered temples, inscriptions on bricks of Nineveh, huge stone gates standing amidst the tropical verdure of Yucatan, Etruscan wine-jars now dry and empty forever.

Ours are the old credulities. With us are Wotan, Zeus, Ormuzd, Isis, Vishnu.

From us comes that miasm of inertia that holds humanity in thrall; from us comes the strength of war-makers, monarchs, and all the privileged.

We reach up long, sinewy, gray arms of custom and tradition, to choke Today and impede Tomorrow.

We are the world's Yesterdays. If you knew enough to put your feet upon us you might rise rapidly. But when you let us ride on your backs we strangle and smother you.

I am Yesterday. Learn to look me in the face, to use me, and not to be afraid of me.

I am not your friend. I am your judge—and your fear.

Tomorrow is your friend.

About the Author

Dr. Frank Crane (1861–1928) was a Presbyterian minister, a speaker, and a popular columnist. Newspapers throughout the eastern United States carried his column around the turn of the century, and in 1919 he published the ten volumes set of *Four Minute Essays*. He published various other works, most notably *Everyday Wisdom*. After his death, his words slowly faded from the public view, and today only tidbits of his works have survived as quotes scattered throughout books, speeches, and websites.

Index

A

B

C